24

*What Can
Happen
in a Day*

Michael Ford Jr.

Promise Land Publishing

24
What Can Happen in A Day
All Rights Reserved.
Copyright © 2018 Michael Ford Jr.
v4.0

Promise Land Publishing

ISBN: 978-0-578-20552-6

Library of Congress Control Number: 2018948136

Illustrations © 2018 James Shipley. All rights reserved - used with permission.
Author Photo © 2018 Shantel Pettway. All rights reserved - used with permission.

Outskirts Press and the "OP" logo are trademarks belonging to Outskirts Press, Inc.

PRINTED IN THE UNITED STATES OF AMERICA

Dedications

I dedicate this book to my Lord and Savior Jesus Christ for blessing me with such an honorable and adventurous profession, and for His protection of all the brave men and women that serve their communities as firefighters and first responders, and all of the staff and family members who support them.

I dedicate this book to all the men and women that I served with during my 23-year career in the Louisville Fire Department, and especially Chief Gregory Fredrick who showed great confidence in me.

I dedicate this book to my wife and high school sweetheart Andrea, and to my sons and daughters who were always my motivation and inspiration.

I dedicate this book to my mother Wanda and father Michael Sr., who always encouraged and prayed for me, and whom I always endeavored to make proud.

I dedicate this book to my siblings Melissa, Mark, Scott, Candice, Shannon, John, Joy, Michelle, Stephen, Cory, Nicole, Larry, Shandy, Kim & Tonia.

Note from the Author

Names, dates, places, and incidents in this book have been changed. Any resemblance to anyone living or dead is purely coincidental.

Table of Contents

INTRODUCTION
"Anything Can Happen in 24 Hours"

In late winter of 1994, I marched into the office of the Assistant Chief of the Louisville Fire Department to interview for a job. I had on my pin-striped blue suit with my solid red necktie, a white button-down French-cuffed shirt with a pair of gold cuff links, and to top it all off, I was walking in my dad's black highly polished wingtip church shoes. That's right, I was in my full power suit! Clean-shaven, too; I was here to impress, I was here for the job. I was twenty years old, a physical specimen of manliness, and with the ego to match. Here I was, going after one of the most coveted and respected professions on the planet, and in Louisville, a great-paying job with benefits. As I stepped through the interview door, I put on my championship smile, mainly to hide the fear and trepidation raging within me.

I stuck out my hand to the assistant chief. "Good morning, sir. My name is Michael Ford, and I'm here to become a firefighter."

That old cuss just stared me down with utter contempt and disgust, as if he was trying to peer into my soul to see all of my inner workings. And without shaking my hand, he said sternly, "Just sit down!"

Now, every piece of real confidence and every ounce of the fake poise and self-assurance that I was trying to exude was fast escaping from my body, seeping through my pores in the form of perspiration. Just as I was destined to sink into the folds of this chair like the Titanic sank into the Atlantic, the other interviewer that was sitting behind the desk, a female with the rank of major, gave me the most beautiful, reassuring, sun on a cloudy day smile. Without words, she told me, "Calm down, everything will be just fine." And on that note, the interview began.

The assistant chief and the major both asked me quite a number of open-ended questions; you know--describe your strengths and weaknesses; how well do you work in a team; what would you do in this or that situation; etc. And I was, without trying to be too braggadocious, knocking these questions clear out of the park. The southern charm had kicked in and I was finally winning them over to my side.

All of a sudden, that old chief asked me a question that I hadn't properly thought through. He said, "Michael, why do you want to be a fireman? And don't give me that bull-crap about how you've dreamed about being a fireman since you were a baby!"

So I pondered for a minute. I thought, *This guy isn't going to allow me to give him some simpleton answer off the top of my head like "I just need a good job."* No, this question actually required some introspection. Why did this profession interest me? It was true that I hadn't wanted to be a fireman all of my life.

I flashed back over the last two years of my life since graduating from high school. I have been working in the local air packaging hub, sorting and loading packages into these white igloo containers all day, five days a week. It was a job that paid just above minimum wage. Though it was good, honest work, it lacked purpose; it was repetitive, routine, unimaginative; it was downright boring. Every person that I worked with hated their job; they absolutely despised the smell of the place. Even I found it to be a genuine chore to come in every day.

Then, "eureka," it hit me. There were five firemen who were members of the same church that I attended. These guys, at some time over the past two years, had encouraged me to apply for the fire department. In every conversation, each of them would highlight the particular segments of the job that they enjoyed the most.

Firefighter Eric told me about how dangerous the job was, the sheer adrenaline rush that comes when that bell sounds, sliding down a pole from the 2nd floor, racing to the fire truck, donning a full set of gear in less than a minute, jumping in the truck, legally speeding down any street, pulling up to a house that has flames pouring out of the windows, crowds of people screaming, and you have been trained and prepared to save the day.

Firefighter Melvyn explained to me how going to work at the firehouse is like coming home. When you arrive, there will be a group of men and women there, "family," whom you are going to spend the rest of the day and night with, laughing, joking, eating, playing, and eventually going into battle with. You will mourn personal loss together, and you will celebrate every personal win together.

Firefighter Billy enlightened me concerning the serious commitment to service involved in being a fireman. "You are going to find yourself in some tough spots, where that fire and heat are laying down on top of you, and your inner voice will question why in the world you signed up for this? The thing that will keep you going is your commitment to saving lives, and your commitment to being there for your firefighter brothers and sisters."

When I listened to these guys talk about their job, it was unlike anything that I had ever heard. I mean really, when was the last time you heard someone boast about how much they loved their job? When was the last time somebody told you, "I can't wait to get to work each day" and was genuinely enthusiastic and proud of the work they do daily? I realized that something was very special about this firefighting gig. After hearing from these guys, I was almost convinced, but not yet. I wasn't fully persuaded until Firefighter Jason gave it to me simple and plain.

"Michael," he said, "most people hate their jobs for one reason--their job is meaningless and boring! They do the same thing every single day for thirty or forty years; the monotony is killing them. Michael, do you want to know what makes the fire department so great?"

I was thinking, *Yeah, hurry up and tell me.*

Then he said something that really stimulated my young and impressionable mind. "We work a 24-hour shift, one day at work and two days off. And Michael, in those 24 hours, anything can happen!"

I interrupted. "What do you mean, anything?"

He continued, "In the fire department there are no two days alike. Every day is different and will present new incidents, diverse challenges, and an array of issues that will stretch and broaden you as a human being. You will see and experience situations that are so strange and out of the ordinary that most people couldn't even imagine! The fire profession is an adventure!"

As all of this flashed through my memory in an instant, I answered the old chief. "Yes, I want to be a fireman so that I can help people, and because it pays well, because of the brotherhood, but mostly because I want to be able to come to work each morning with the excitement and nervousness of the unknown, the thrill of facing extraordinary circumstances, and knowing that today, in these 24 hours, anything can happen!

That old chief cracked a crooked smile at me, as he sat on the other side of his desk, and said, "Mr. Ford, that's why I'm still here." And with that, he stood up, and shook my hand. A few weeks later I received an offer of employment letter in the mail, stating that I was to start the Fire Academy in April.

CHAPTER 1
My First Day

In the spring of 1995, I was officially initiated into the professional fire service. I was to report to the Fire Training Academy at 0800 hours (that's 8 a.m. for you civilians). What a terrific morning! Yesterday I was a lowly package handler (nothing wrong with that), but today, I am a 21-year-old professional firefighter. I am a distinguished man in the community, on top of the world, the cream of the crop, the image of Courage, Duty, Dedication, Honor (the Louisville Fire motto). As I arrive and stroll from the parking lot toward the Academy, trying to take it all in, a fine older gentleman in his fire department uniform, with his gold badge glistening in the early morning sun, is holding the door open for me. I think, *Wow, this Academy stuff is really going to be nice.*

As I get closer to the entrance, that fine gentleman yells out at me and the young man walking directly behind me, "Hey, you stupid freakin new boys--run your butts in here; you are freakin late!" (He actually used a more derogatory word than freakin.) As I start into a complete run toward the door, I look at my watch and confirm that I am actually forty minutes early. So when I come through the door I respond to the gentleman that it was my understanding that we were to report to the Academy at 0800 hours, and that it was just now 7:20 a.m. He responds with, "New Boy, this is the fire department; if you want to show up at your own pace, then go be a mailman. Around here, you are to be in your seat at least an hour before 0800 hours."

As I hurry to find my assigned seat among the thirty other recruits, I try to brush off this first fire department mishap. While I am working to get myself settled, somebody hollers from the rear of the room, "Everybody up!" Immediately, everyone in the room stands to attention as our commanding officer walks into the room. Captain T, is a gigantic, 6-foot-5-inch man with a bullhorn in his throat. He might as well be Mr. T, because he has the ominous, intimidating presence to match. Captain T stands behind the podium and with his softest voice he makes the hair of the two recruits sitting directly in front of me stand up on their heads as if they are riding on the expressway in a convertible.

He begins his first speech to us by explaining to us just how brainless and unintelligent all of us are; how he considers it a miracle of God that we all have made it one whole hour without already being fired. He goes on to clarify how and why none of us are worthy to be called firemen, let alone Louisville Firemen. As he points his giant finger at all of us he says, "Don't you dare tell another person in this community that you are a fireman; you are not firemen, you are just recruits! If you survive the next five and a half months of this academy, then you will be a Louisville Firefighter."

That's when he notices that some of the guys have purchased some fire department t-shirts and worn them to class. Captain T blows up! "Take those shirts off right now," he says, as now all of our hairs are standing up in the wind of his voice. So from that day forward, we wear jerseys that just have a number on them. I am no longer Michael; my new name is Red 4, or "New Boy" for short. This morning I felt so proud and professional, but now "UPS package handler" seems so much more respectable. And like [1]Dorothy, in the Wizard of Oz, I realize I'm not in Kansas anymore; this fire department stuff is going to be extremely challenging.

Immediately following the morning address and all of the personnel introductions, Captain T informs us that there is someone special he wants to introduce us to before we go any further in the day. The other training officers scream at us to get up, and they march us quickly outside to the large five-story concrete training tower. We stand at attention as Captain T walks up to the front to address all of us. He says with an evil grin to the thirty recruits, "New Boys, I want to introduce you all to the Plum Lady; you will be spending a lot of quality time with her. I want you two to get well acquainted."

We all look with a great deal of bewilderment as he gently strokes this attached, seven- story, faded purple, metal ladder, that goes straight up the side of the building. Uh-oh. I understand. The Plum Lady is their first form of torturing us. Captain T states that this "Lady" is going to teach us how to properly ascend and descend tall buildings. For some reason, my [2]Spider Man senses have me feeling like the [3]Karate Kid in

---

1   (LeRoy, 8/25/1939)
2   (Ditko, 1962)
3   (Weintraub, 1984)

Mr. Miyagi's back yard. I think we're about to do a lot of "Wax on, and wax off" before we actually learn how to fight fire.

Sure enough, Captain T screams, "Alright boys, up and over!" Just before we begin our ascent, the training officers blow up a large red and yellow safety airbag and place it next to the building. It's about 12 feet wide and 12 feet long; it's a so-called safety measure, to catch us if we happen to slip and fall. "Don't you New Boys get any ideas about falling off this ladder and this airbag catching you! It's only rated for a fall of up to the three stories, and you are going up past the seventh floor, and on to the roof!" Captain T shouts.

I am among the first group to go up and over. The first time up is refreshing, even a bit exhilarating. Hey, climbing tall buildings, this is real fireman stuff. But the second and third time up, not so much; your thighs really start to burn, your breathing is a little more labored, and your forearms really begin to cramp. Then Captain T says, "Two more times!" Now, my back, my hands, my feet, and my shoulders join the other parts of my body that are screaming for relief, and I am no longer sure I put antiperspirant under my arms. "Alright, Red Team--that's enough, next group," whistles Captain T.

None too soon, either; I don't think I could have climbed one more rung. The yellow team starts up for their first climb. As they near the top of the Plum Lady, their progress comes to a complete stop. Captain T hollers, "What the hell is the holdup, Yellow Team?" There he is, Yellow 8, scared to death as he hugs with both arms the 5th-floor section of the Plum Lady ladder. He won't say a word, even as all of the training officers and the other recruits try to encourage him to continue. Then without warning, Yellow 8 pushes off the rails of the

Plum Lady and swan-dives backwards off the 5th-floor section of the tower! Everything was so still and quiet, you could have heard a rat licking ice. I would like to tell you that it was like he fell in slow motion, but a man falling five stories happens in a blink of an eye.

Yellow 8 smashes into that airbag, you know, the one that is only rated for a fall of up to the third floor. He totally collapses that bag! All the training officers scurry over to unravel the airbag that has wrapped around him, and to see if he is still alive. Do you remember how when you were young and did something really dumb that could have really hurt you, how worried your parents were? Until the moment they realize that you are alright--then they want to kill you. That's how this is. Those training officers surely feel the weight of responsibility on their shoulders. Will they have a recruit killed on the first day of training? No, Yellow 8 has survived, unscathed from a fifth floor backwards decent off of the Plum Lady. Unbelievable! What is also unbelievable in that moment is all the colorful, descriptive names that the training officers are able to conjure up to describe their feelings of Yellow 8. I think, *This guy is surely fired*, but after they have given him a good cussing, they inquire why he jumped. Yellow 8 says that he jumped because he was afraid of heights. Apparently, this guy has not properly researched his chosen profession, which shouldn't have been too hard to do. A five-year-old can tell you that firemen climb ladders!

Well, Captain T grabs Yellow 8 by the shoulders and says, "Son, do you want to be a fireman?"

Yellow 8 nods his head in agreement. "Then get back in line with your group, and the next time you fall off a ladder, you better have a rung in your hand or you can consider yourself fired before you hit the ground!"

Yellow 8 says, "Yes, sir" and jogs back to his place in line to go back over the Plum Lady. The training officers set the airbag back up, and Yellow Team ascends upward. Now everyone's eyes are fixed on Yellow 8--surely he'll make it this time. As he approaches the fifth floor, he begins to moan, and shake, and shouts out, "I can't do it!" And just like before, he just lets go and falls backwards off the Plum Lady, this time taking Yellow 9 Recruit with him as they both crash into the inflated airbag.

This time, the officers are especially worried; they have never had two guys land on the safety airbag simultaneously. They sprint over to check on both guys--fortunately, that safety airbag performed at a higher level than it was rated. Both recruits are unharmed, but visibly shaken. Which is quite understandable; I am not one of the recruits that fell five stories off the side of the building, but I'm shaken and a bit disturbed. As Yellow 8 stands up, you can see the tears streaming down his face. He knows his lifelong dream and vision of being a fireman is finished in less than 24 hours on the job. We all watch as Captain T puts his long arm on Yellow 8's shoulder and slowly walks him inside. It is the last time we see Yellow 8. This moment reminds me of the fact that sometimes in life, everything you've hoped and worked for can be lost in just one day. I realize that the only way I am going to successfully complete the fire academy is to face each challenge with great tenacity and tremendous effort.

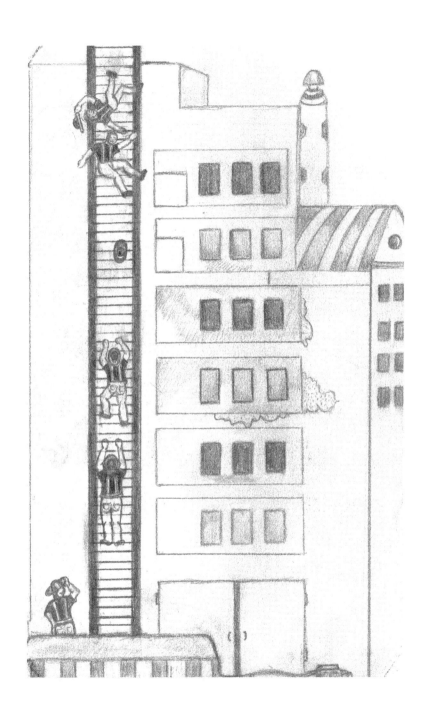

CHAPTER 2
Fire Academy

I would love to report to you that my ensuing days in the fire academy were a glorious success, but honestly my training days were a little stormier than sunny. Upon arriving for my second day of drill school (nearly two hours early this time), I am called over to the Fire Officers' coffee table by Sgt. Spade. "Red 4, come here!" Now Sgt. Spade had nearly twenty-five years on the fire department; he is about 5'5" feet tall, with a belly that makes him look seven months pregnant. He looks the opposite of what you think of when you think of a firefighter. He is probably only about fifty years old, but to a twenty-one year-old, he might as well have been ninety years old, because he just looks decrepit.

I quickly move toward the table. "Yes, sir--how can I help you, sir?"

Sgt. Spade says, "Come closer, New Boy." Sgt. Spade pulls me closer, as if he has a secret that he wants to share with me. He says, "New Boy, I really don't like you, and as far as I'm concerned, you might as well quit, because I plan on firing you before this academy is over."

As his moist, foul, disgusting coffee-and-cigarette-stained breath is hitting the side of my nose and cheek, I'm wondering what I did in one day to make this man hate me and cause him to promise that he is going to work to fire me.

> **{LESSON 1} "In this life, some people will not like or appreciate you. They may not like your smile, your face, your gender, your personality, or your history, but never allow their issues to divert or thwart you from achieving your goals!"**

Sgt. Spade reminds me of his threat on a daily basis, and unfortunately, I allow Sgt. Spade's verbal harassment and threats to cause me additional and unnecessary anxiety. There are times when the recruits are learning some new skill or technique, and I am doing well until Sgt. Spade makes his way over to stand next to me just to get me flustered.

Let me ask you a question. Have you ever had somebody that agitated and constantly tried to push your buttons? You know how when you are in that person's presence and your thoughts have a tendency to wander into some violent daydreaming moment where you're smacking that person all around the room and really teaching them a good lesson on why they shouldn't be perturbing you. Anyway, that's how I feel every time Sgt. Spade comes near me. This too is causing me to be unfocused and off my game. I begin to realize that this man has no power to fire me; that is why he is working so hard to provoke me to quit. Many times, your adversary can't beat you, so he will work to frustrate you and incite you to self-destruct.

{LESSON 2} "Use your adversary's negativity to fuel your fire to succeed!"

Nearly six weeks into a very arduous and challenging Fire Academy, the competitor in me awakes. I make up in my mind that I will not allow this man to cause me to abort my dream and my mission to become a member of the Louisville Fire and Rescue.

One Monday morning, Captain T gives all of the recruits an order to bring swim trunks tomorrow because we all will be transported to a local High School for the mandatory swim test.

Oh no, not a swim test; I'm in serious trouble! I knew that the firefighter application required for the applicant to be able to swim as a mandatory condition to pass your one-year probation, but no one had mentioned it since. I thought that my secret was safe. I know you've guessed already. That's right, I couldn't swim. Tuesday morning arrives, seemingly quicker than usual. We all load the thirty-year-old red Fire Department bus and proceed to the high school. Twenty-eight of the now twenty-nine recruits get dressed into their swim trunks and gleefully cannonball into the pool. The last remaining recruit (yours truly) takes his time and gently tiptoes down the small ladder into the water, and holds ever so gently to the base of the ladder to ensure that my feet can actually touch the bottom of the pool. As of yet, my secret is still safe.

Captain T explains that the swim test is simple; just one lap up and back the length of the pool and you pass. One recruit shouts out, "Are we being timed?" Another asks, "Does it matter what style you swim?" Captain T responds that it isn't timed, and it doesn't matter what style you employ, as long as your feet don't touch the bottom. "Are you ready?" he shouts. "Go!"

There is this massive combination of bubbles of water and twenty-eight young men frantically racing through the water to get to the other side; their pace is fierce. Then there is me, waddling slowly through the water with one hand pinching my nose, one arm spinning me in a circle, and my legs propelling splashes of water in every direction. I have my eyes closed, but in my mind, I think I am traveling in the same bunch as the other twenty-eight recruits. I really think I am getting somewhere. By the time I stop thrashing around, everyone has completed their lap, and I have only traveled about ten feet sideways.

Captain T hollers, "Mr. Ford, get out of the pool!" He asks me, "Mr. Ford, why don't you know how to swim?"

I explain to him that this is only the second time that I have ever been in a real pool. The first time was in high school on a field trip where I almost drowned because I didn't know that just because one end of the pool says four feet doesn't mean that the other end isn't twelve feet deep.

He says, "Mr. Ford, there weren't any pools in your neighborhood?"

I further explain to him that in my neighborhood there were no real swimming pools. We had a park that was near us, which had a water sprinkler that would spray water and collect the water in a basin that was only about two feet deep.

We thought swimming was when you went and lay on the concrete under the stream of water and flapped your arms around like a bird.

Captain T interrupts my explanation, "Mr. Ford, you must learn how to swim or you will be fired."

A little while later, my adversary finds me alone and reminds me that I should just quit before I'm embarrassingly fired. Before Sgt. Spade spoke those negative words, I was truly discouraged, but his negative words seem to ignite a fire into my weakening resolve. Something in me abhors the thought of giving this man the satisfaction of being right. I look him in the eye with the most ferocious look that I can muster and declare to him, with my finger in his face, "You better fire me if you can, because—I—WILL—NEVER--QUIT!!! Sgt. Spade looks surprised, but he just grins and softly walks away. He never harasses me again.

I spend many hours and days training to learn how to swim. I have many great guys and ladies working to teach me how to swim, but to no avail. Firefighter Pears works at a local hotel and allows me to come to the hotel and spend countless hours in the pool. David, a recruit in my academy class, has a girlfriend that works at another hotel, and he spends several hours with me, trying to train me to swim. Nothing seems to work.

One day I am in the pool and a little boy jumps into the lane beside me. He tells his dad, "I don't want to swim on my tummy because the water keeps getting in my nose."

Dad replies very nonchalantly, "Okay boy, just swim on your back."

Epiphany! The reason why I'm having trouble swimming is because the water keeps getting in my nose, and my new surrogate dad just told me to swim on my back. I practice this for the rest of the day and realize that I am a fantastic backstroke swimmer. "Yeah, I can swim!" I feel like a six-year-old that just learned to ride his bike. "Look at me, everybody, I can swim!

Finally, the day comes for me to receive my second and final opportunity to pass the swim test. All the training officers are there, including my adversary. I get in the water and position myself to swim on my back.

Someone asks, "Are you going to swim on your back?"

As I'm pushing off the wall on my back, I smile and say, "You said any style."

I can swim fast, but I decide to take my sweet time and enjoy this accomplishment. Before you know it, I successfully swim up and back, but as I am coming near to the wall, I can see my adversary standing on the side of the pool watching me come to the finish line. I gleam and smile right at him as I smoothly drift to the finish line wall.

Captain T says, "Well, that's a Louisville Fire Department first; I've never seen anyone complete the test on their back before."

I think, *Yes! I've only been here for a brief time, and I'm already making my mark.* This is my final obstacle; it's official, and I'm now an actual member of the Louisville Fire Department. Everyone is excited for me—I think, even my adversary.

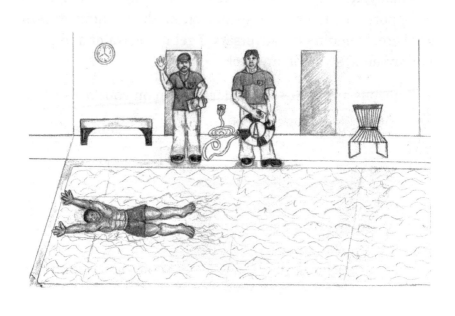

CHAPTER 3
Training Days

In order to graduate what may be one of the most strenuous and demanding Fire Academies in the country, every Louisville Fire Recruit must complete a rigorous four hundred hours of fire training and sixty hours of emergency medical training. I need to really highlight this fact before moving on to share some of the awe-inspiring events that I have seen and experienced as a twenty-three-year firefighter. In my later years on the department, I have spent a number of years recruiting all over the community for individuals to apply for the fire department. Everywhere that I went, people would say, "I could never be a firefighter, they run into burning buildings, they carry the Jaws of Life, they are super brave!" But the truth is, the most amazing thing about firefighters is they are not supernatural beings; they are just regular people that have been trained to serve their community at an extremely high level.

The six months of fire recruit training included: Firefighter Orientation and Safety – Fire Behavior – Rescue and Extrication – Forcible Entry and Ground Ladders – Ventilation

– Waters Supply – Fire Suppression – Communications - Building Construction for Fire Suppression Forces - Domestic Preparedness - Weapons of Mass Destruction - Basic Fire Prevention Education - Fire Arson Detection - Noncombustible and Fire-Resistive Building Construction

Each morning of drill school, the instructors have the recruits stand and recite the [4]Pledge of Allegiance to the US Flag. Immediately following, a firefighter is chosen to sing the national anthem, and everyone is "blessed" with at least one turn, no matter how dreadful their vocals. Next, someone is chosen to give a "Word of the Day." The "Word of the Day" normally consists of words such as "Honor, Pride, Commitment, Perseverance, Trust, Community, Brotherhood, Family, Integrity," words that speak to the desired character of a firefighter. But one particular morning, Captain T interrupts and says that he has the "Word for Today."

"Today's word is "Resignation," he says very calmly. As we all look around waiting for some explanation of this odd word, he announces, "Today's training exercise will cause some to decide firefighting isn't for you, and if that's the case, I'm accepting all resignations."

Now there is a palpable level of distress in the room. I mean, what can he be talking about? We have already been in the academy for four months; we've been in and on top of burning buildings, endured hours of the "Plum Lady," sat in a smoke-filled room with no mask on while tears streamed down our faces from the intensity of the smoke. What else could they throw at us that could be so terrifying to cause us

---

4   (Balch, 1954)

to quit now? While we ponder, Captain T shouts, "Get your gear on and meet me outside!"

We arrive to what we call the incident scene, and there lies a fifty-foot, three splice (sectioned) metal ladder, which has four Kernmantle ropes attached to the top. I shake my head. I'm thinking, *I don't know what this is, but I don't like it.* I watch as all of our instructors have evil, disgusting grins on their faces, as if they are quietly excited, this can only mean something truly unpleasant for us recruits.

"In the event of a church or an auditorium fire, we may need to penetrate a very high ceiling," Captain T begins to explain. "So the evolution that you are about to perform is called the auditorium ladder raise."

The auditorium ladder raise consists of four firefighters raising the fifty-foot ladder, which weighed nearly 350lbs, straight up in the air. These four firefighters are to be assisted by four additional firemen that are to hold and pull the attached ropes in order to bring some level of stability to the 350-pound ladder that is standing straight up. Finally, the real problem.

"Every one of you will climb all the way up to the top of one side of the ladder, place your leg over the top rung, and come down the other side, or you can officially give me your resignation," Captain T states, clear and resolute. He then asks, "Who wants to go first!"

Now I would love to uphold the aura of bravery that firefighters usually possess and tell you that we all fight each other for the chance to go first. But you have to understand, we had all struggled just raising and holding that 50-foot ladder for the few seconds it takes to raise it and lay it on the side of a building. Plus, climbing a 50-foot ladder that's at an angle is difficult enough, but one that is standing straight up is just wrong!

"Fat Boy should go first!" shouts Sgt. Spade. He is referring to Yellow 5, a recruit that had come into the academy overweight. Just like I had to learn to swim or be fired, he had to lose a significant amount of weight or be fired. Captain T yells, "Recruit Hud, you're up!" Now though I feel bad for my friend, I feel more relieved that my name wasn't called. Actually, this isn't a bad choice. I mean, if Yellow 5 can make it up without falling or being dropped by the guys holding the ladder, then maybe all of us can do it.

As we hold the ladder, Yellow 5 starts his slow trek up the ladder, and I begin to worry. *What if he falls? He won't be the only one killed; he'll fall and smash me in the process!* He takes a good while to get to the top, and everyone that is holding the ladder is wishing he would hurry, because he's heavy! Of course, each of us will soon get our turn and none of us will feel the sensation to hurry. Yellow 5 makes it down safely, and everyone cheers. A few others go up and over, and it's beginning to lose its fear factor. It's my turn, and I'm feeling fairly confident. I climb up the first 20-foot section with ease, but I get to the next 15-foot section and notice that the second section diminishes in width. No problem; I just take it a bit slower. I get to the third 15-foot section and realize that the width diminishes even further. Now I'm clutching the rungs and pressing my body to the ladder, looking like a baby crawling, when I hear my adversary holler, "Ford, if you fall, don't think your family is getting any benefits! As far as I'm concerned, you're fired before you hit the ground!" I can't allow my adversary to see me fail, so I press on.

I get to the top and look around. Unfortunately, I can see the entire city skyline, and as the ladder is gently swaying in the wind, I must now pull my leg over to the other side of the ladder. I quickly ponder if doing this dangerous job, placing my life on the line, is really what I want to do with my life, and for a moment I gave great thought about this morning's "Word of the Day."

{LESSON 3} "Life has a way of presenting situations that look like they're too far up to climb. But just take one step at a time, even if you have to clutch real hard and crawl like a baby, and you will eventually find yourself on your way over the top."

I decide at that moment, *Yes, this is what I want to do with my life*. I make it up and over to the other side. As a matter of fact, all of us recruits make it, and none of us are compelled to use the "Word of the Day."

CHAPTER 4
Lights and Sirens!

The Louisville Fire Department's training academy is focused on preparing the new fire recruit for the unexpected challenges they will face on their 24-hour tour of duty. So each day that we arrive at the academy, we have no idea what our torturers--I mean, our training officers-- are going to throw at us. Don't get me wrong; we know everyday is a "Plum Lady" day and a two-mile run, but the rest is a surprise. This morning as I arrive, my name is called; it is announced that I am to complete a day of ambulance ride time. All the recruits are in the middle of our twelve weeks of Emergency Medical Technician (EMT) training. Every one of us will be required to complete sixteen hours of actual ambulance ride time as part of our medical emergency training.

I finish my morning fire recruit routine, grab my brown paper lunch bag, and head over to the awaiting ambulance. I am greeted by the two crew members, Mike (a thirteen-year veteran paramedic) and Julia (a nine-year veteran EMT). "Grab the back jump seat and get buckled in, we've just received a run!" Mike says with a big smile on his face.

[run = emergency incident = 911 emergency call]

I step up into the back of the ambulance, where my backward-facing seat has the view of just the back door. I'm not really nervous, nor excited. I mean, it's not a building on fire; it's probably just some person with a headache. Then, the emergency lights come on and sirens start to whoop, and now the big smile that was on Mike's face is transferred to me. This is my first time riding with the lights, sirens, the speeding, and busting through red lights. We are forcing cars to scurry to each side of the road to allow us through--I mean, we are parting the road like Moses parted the waters at the Red Sea. Now I'm excited! Now I know that whenever these lights and sirens turn on it's going to mean fun and excitement for me.

We pull up on the scene; there is an old, faded, lime-green 1930s shotgun house. There is a police officer waiting for us at the door. As we park, Mike hollers at me from the front seat, "New Boy [New Boy is the name every new recruit is called for at least their first year on the department], grab the red medical bag."

The three of us rush to the front door, and truly I don't know what to expect, but Mike and Julia have their game faces on, so I put mine on too. As we come through the door, we find a young lady in her early twenties lying on the old splintered wood floor. She is in pain and covered in her own blood. Mike asks her, "What happened?"

She painfully opens her mouth where her lips are puffed up and teeth covered in dried blood. She tells us that some man knocked on the side door, and when she asked who it was, the man kicked the door in. I turn and give a quick glance backwards to see the door. Earlier, when we came through that door, I didn't notice that it was just dangling on its hinges. The young lady continues, "The door smacked me in the face, and I fell to the floor. The next thing I know, there was a man sitting on top of me beating me in my face with his fist. I think I blacked out for a minute; when I came to, he had pulled my pants down."

She gasps and pauses as her voice just crumbles, and tears work their way through her eyelids that are black and purple and completely swollen shut. Her home has been invaded; she has been beaten and raped. There is a picture of a very beautiful girl on the mantel over the old fireplace; it is of this young lady before this horrific attack that she just endured. We get her semi-cleaned up and packaged (packaged = wounds bandaged, extremities immobilized, placed on the stretcher, ready for transport to emergency room). As we head to the the hospital, I sit in the back with paramedic Mike as he puts in an IV line and a bag of fluids. The young lady lies quietly on the stretcher, and yet I can see the pupils of her eyes peering out at me through the mush of her battered face. I am truly overwhelmed with emotions. I'm thinking, *This could have been my girlfriend, or one of my sisters.* I just turned twenty-one and I'm thinking, *This stuff really goes on in the world? There are really people this cruel and this brutal?* I don't know the patient/emergency worker protocols yet, but I can't help myself; this girl, who is about my age, has just experienced about the wickedest thing that could ever happen to a person, and she is alone, with no family's love to surround her. So I reach out and grasp her hand, just to share my sympathies, my support, to maybe sit where her loved ones would sit if they were here. She doesn't say anything; she just embraces my hand tightly all the rest of the way to the hospital.

After a few minutes of down-time (down-time is the time between emergency incidents) Mike tells us to load up because we have a run in the south end of Louisville. So here we go again, lights and sirens. This time when the lights and sirens come on, there is no smile on my face, no joy in my heart; I am just wondering what this incident could be. Finally, we pull up to a corner of a busy intersection, where there is a sixty-year-old man sitting on the ground with his middle-aged daughter.

Mike asks the man, "What's going on today?"

The older gentleman responds, "Well, I feel a little weak and I have some fluttering in my chest."

Mike tells me to grab the EKG monitor off the truck (EKG monitor is a device that tracks the heart and gives an electric shock to a person's heart in order to make it beat normally). We open the man's shirt and begin to attach the EKG leads/wires to the man's chest. Mike asks the man, "Are you in pain?"

"No, I'm not in any pain," the man explains.

Mike reads the squiggly lines on the monitor and tells the man that his heart is in defibrillation. Then Mike says something that I will never forget. "Sir, I'm going to have to shock you."

I'm thinking, *What? Can you shock a man that is up talking to you? I've never seen this kind of stuff in the movies, and nobody ever mentioned this in class!*

Mike says calmly to the man, "Sir, THIS IS GOING TO HURT."

Wow, what an understatement. Mike lays the man on his back and rubs those two silver hand paddles together--you know, like you've seen in all the old doctors' TV shows, and he says, "Everybody clear!"

That means step back and don't touch the patient, so that you are not shocked or electrocuted in the process. Mike presses the paddles to the old man's chest, and "POW!" nearly 700 volts of electricity pass into this man's heart! The old man goes unconscious, and the squiggly line that we saw on the monitor earlier ain't squiggly anymore! It is just a straight, flat line! That means our patient is dead. I'm trying to play it cool so as not to let the daughter feel like there is a problem, but I know my face is telling the whole story! My mouth is sitting wide open, my eyes are all bugged out, and I'm thinking Mike just killed this man, a man that was up talking no more than a minute ago. Oh my God! I'm thinking I am an accomplice to a murder; now I'm worried that we are not just going to be fired, but that we are probably both going to jail for this one!

Mike hollers again, "Clear!" POW! He shocks the old man again. This time the old man comes up off the ground, swinging and flailing his arms and screaming in pain. Mike smiles, and says calmly, "There we go, all better now."

Easy for him to say. I need to change my shirt, and maybe my underwear. Any more of this excitement, and I might need Mike to hit me with a few volts! Well, we package the man up and transport him to the nearest hospital.

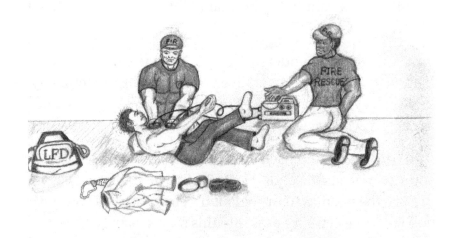

The rest of that that day, we respond to a few more incidents, most not worth writing about. As we are driving down the street, Mike says, "Well, New Boy that's about it for your first day of ambulance ride time; let's get you back to the Academy."

"Yes, sir, that sounds good to me."

But no sooner than I say that, the radio (radio = communication or 911 center, or dispatch) calls for our unit to respond to a woman vomiting blood. Once again, the lights and sirens come on. Once again, we grab the equipment and the stretcher. When we come to the door, it is already open, so we enter a beautiful and expensive house, where everything is orderly and pristine.

The voice in the other room faintly says, "I'm in here."

We walk into the great-room/family room and there is an attractive older woman lying on the couch. I consider her older from my twenty-one-year-old perspective, but in actuality she is only in her late thirties. She's pretty, but she has an obvious look of being sick. EMT Julia asks her what's wrong. The lady says that she's been nauseous and vomiting blood. Mike tells me to take the woman's vitals (vitals = patient's blood pressure, pulse rate, respirations, oxygen level, sometimes sugar level). I kneel down next to the woman and as I'm holding her arm to get her vitals, she announces that she has HIV...AIDS. AIDS, did she just say AIDS?! I look up over to Mike, to see if I can catch a glimpse of his reaction to this revelation. I mean, what's the protocol for this? Should I be touching this lady's arm? Should I be holding my breath so that I don't breathe in her cooties! Okay, folks; don't be too mad at me--don't judge me too harshly without considering the times. I just turned twenty-one, it's the mid-'90s, AIDS is still a big bad ugly wolf in the world, I'm a few weeks into my training, and I am in no way a professional.

I quickly finish her vitals and as we package her for transport, I'm thinking this is a good time to ask to drive the ambulance to the hospital, you know, to get some experience. But before I can spring my cowardly plan into action, Mike says, "New Boy, I'm going to let you handle this one in the back all by yourself."

"What?" I say softly as I give Mike my most worried and scared look.

Mike tells me that there is nothing that he can do for her, because she is not in any pain, she isn't dehydrated, and her vitals are good. He reassures me that I can handle it. He tells me to just take her vitals again and start filling out the paperwork (paperwork is official documents/incident forms). As we're driving off, I begin to take her vitals for the second time. Neither of us is saying anything. I sit back in my seat and begin filling out the paperwork, when I notice the lady crying. Tears are rapidly flowing down her face, so I ask, "Ma'am, are you hurting? Are you in pain?"

She answers me, "Just my heart." She then begins to inform me that she had been married to her husband for eighteen years, and before she had met him she had not been with any other person (I had assumed that she meant in the biblical sense). She continues, "I've been faithful to him." She pauses. "I started getting sick, and the doctors finally determined that I had HIV/AIDS. I told them that was impossible, because I don't sleep around. The doctors were silent, and when I looked at my husband, his face told the rest of the story. He had been cheating on me for years. They tested him--he has HIV, but not AIDS." She shakes her head in disbelief. She says, "But that's not why I'm hurting. I have two young boys that will have to grow up without their mother. They don't deserve that." She closes her eyes, and the tears begin to stream down her face.

In that moment, I receive some clarity,

> **{LESSON 4}** *"I realized that being a fireman was more than just putting water on a fire, that the reason people move out of the way when we are coming through is not because of the brightness of the lights nor the loudness of the siren, but because of the respect the people in the community have for what the firefighters do every day. The respect from all of those that have experienced an*

emergency in their lives and those lights and sirens represented help, support, and comfort to a person in immediate need and distress."

I reach for her hand, the one that just minutes ago I was afraid of, and I hold it with both of my hands. Without saying another word, she presses my hand tightly all the rest of the way. After we arrive at the hospital, as we are transferring her to the nurses at the hospital, the lady releases my hand, looks up at me and says, "Thank you young man."

I smile at her, and as I walk away, I am filled with emotion. I could cry, but I hold it all in.

Over the years I have thought and prayed for that lady and her two boys. I've hoped that she was able to survive, at least until her boys had grown up. I would eventually find out in my time as a fireman, that you enter the most difficult times of people's lives, you're with them for those few trying moments, and then you may never see or hear the end or the rest of that person's story. I learned that day that one of the most important responsibilities of all great firefighters is to lend the **"Ministry of your Presence"** (When no words can comfort, just being there speaks of how much you care) to people during the most challenging times of their lives.

We eventually make it back to the academy past my regular working hours, and all the other recruits have gone home for the day. I get cleaned up and leave for the day. Later on that evening, my girlfriend Andrea stops by the dorm that I am living in to check on me. She greets me with a hug and asks me how my day had gone. With a simple smile, I bow my head a little and shake it from north to south in awe of the day I've just experienced.

She scrunches her nose and eyes and looks at me in disbelief. She says, "What? What can happen in a day?"

CHAPTER 5
My First Firehouse Family

Today has been penciled in my calendar as a day of celebration for the past four months. Today is the last day of the Louisville Fire Academy, Class 170 for those of us that are still left (three out of the thirty didn't make it)! Today is the day that we graduate. Today is the day that we will actually be given a silver Louisville Firefighter badge. Today is the last day that I will be called "Red 4"--my new name will be Firefighter Ford! (Though I would learn later that I'm going to be called everything but Firefighter Ford for at least the next few years.) Most important, today is the day that every recruit will receive their first official assignment. Today each of us will learn with which fire company we will be spending one-third of our lives.

We arrive at the Academy at 7 a.m., as we have done for the past four months. We recite the Pledge of Allegiance, sing the National Anthem, give the "Word of the Day," clean the facility inside and out, climb the "Plum Lady," and run two miles, just as we have done for the past twenty weeks. We complete all our assignments that day with a sense of excitement, pride, and maybe a bit of nostalgia in our hearts. About noon, Captain T called the recruits together, along with all the training staff. He says he just wants to talk to us about what happens when we leave the Academy today. He begins to speak to us in the tone of a father giving his children final instructions before they leave the nest. He tells us to follow our new captain's orders to the letter, because he is the one responsible for watching out for us and making sure we don't get killed out there.

Then he says, "The new company that you are going to be assigned to will become your new family. You will train together, you will work together, you will eat and sleep together, you will play together, you will know their spouses and their kids, you will watch out and protect each other. And together, you and your new Firehouse Family will be responsible for fighting fires and saving lives."

As Captain T is speaking in his very low and methodical voice with the cadence of a preacher, there is a quiet excitement in the room, and a low rumbling enthusiasm in the heart of each recruit. It feels like a football locker-room just before kickoff. While Captain T is delivering final instructions, one of the sergeants walks in from the rear of the room.

"It's here!" he says, waving a piece of paper, interrupting the speech and the ambiance. It is the news all of us have been waiting for, the "Assignment List" that contains the fate of each recruit. Now there are twenty-eight recruits left, and there are twenty-two fire stations that we may be assigned to. Each recruit has thoughts or preferences about which Fire Company he desires to be assigned to. Maybe you will go to a specialty Company--Engine 1 and Engine 5 are hazardous materials response companies; Truck 7 and Engine 11 are structural collapse and trench rescue companies; Truck 1 is a high-angle and water-rescue company. Or you could be like me, a recruit that doesn't have any preferences, but is just thrilled to go anywhere outside of the Academy!

Captain T examines the list, nodding his head in approval of what he's seeing. He can sense that we have all moved to silence, and he is deliberately not saying a word in order to draw out the suspense. Finally, he starts from the top. "Firefighter Terrance –Truck 10, Firefighter Joe – Truck 9, Firefighter Michael, Firefighter Phillip, Firefighter Edward, Firefighter Charles," we are all whooping, hollering and clapping as if we actually know something about these companies, and truly most of us don't know anything about any of them. We are excited just to be assigned to a fire station, and I think we like the fact that Captain T is actually calling us firefighters.

My heart is beginning to pound a little harder--I know my name is coming up. Captain T continues, "Firefighter Michael Ford, assigned to Engine 10." Yes! I'm pumped. I don't know anything about my new company or my new fire station family; I don't even know what part of the city it's located in, but I'm just excited to leave the Fire Academy. After Captain T finishes reading everyone's new assignment, he shares some small facts about each station, its location, its reputation, and any other tidbits he can offer, which we are more than willing to receive. He ends the day by telling us that he is letting us out of our last day at the Academy an hour early. This is so that we could go visit our newly assigned companies, drop off our fire gear and equipment, and meet our new families.

After we give our thanks and our goodbyes to all of our instructors, I load up my vehicle with all of my fire equipment and personal items, and I start the fifteen-minute trek to my new Fire Station. As I am driving, I am extremely eager to meet my new firehouse family. I may only be twenty-one years old, but I have a high regard for family. I was fortunate to be raised in a very loving family with my father, mother, two brothers and two sisters in one small house, with one small bathroom. We played, fought, prayed, laughed, cried, but we did it together. Captain T said my fire station was a "Double House with a District Chief." This means that there are actually two fire companies and the Fire District's Chief is housed in one fire station. There is a total of thirty-six personnel assigned to my station, and twelve individuals assigned to my particular shift. I'm thinking about how growing up with my two brothers and my two sisters was so much fun--how much more fun is it going to be with twelve of us in the house?

I finally turn right at the light, off Southern Parkway and onto Ashland Avenue, and there it is: "Truck 8/Engine 10 Fire Station." She is old and crusty looking, but she's mine. As I'm getting out of my car, my Fire Academy Classmate Firefighter Rod pulls up beside me; he's here to also drop of his fire gear. He has also been assigned to Engine 10, but he will be on a different shift, working with a different set of eleven family members. We walk up to the door together and ring the doorbell. Truck 8 Sergeant Mann opens the old red front door and greets us with a smile. We introduce ourselves, and he says in his country twang, "Come on in, fellas." He says, "You boys wait here, and I'll go call the captain."

While he's gone, we have a chance to take it all in--the sight and smell of the place are intensely unique. The view and the decor are old and dreary-looking, yet not depressing, more nostalgic. The distinctive smell is a concoction of burnt wood, damp clothes, molded ceilings, human sweat, expertly prepared cuisine, fresh coffee, old cigarette butts, and the hint of a sugary dessert. My wife would eventually come to simply call this "The Fire Department Smell."

We hear Sergeant Mann on the house intercom. "Captain Dodd, you have visitors at the front door--two New Boys!"

Sergeant Mann comes back out and tells us Captain Dodd will be down in a minute. I know this is just supposed to be a brief five-minute meeting just to say hello, but I'm smiling, excited to meet my new captain, the guy that will be my Fire Station Dad, the person that will help shape and mold me into an experienced firefighter and eventually push me on to become a distinguished Fire Officer. Captain Dodd comes down the stairs, walks over to me and Firefighter Rod.

I extend my hand, and with a smile I introduce myself. "Good afternoon, sir. I am Firefighter Michael Ford, and I'm your new firefighter."

To my shock, Captain Dodd turns up his face in frustration and refuses to shake my hand; instead he extends his hand to Firefighter Rod, and says, "Rod, I knew your dad; I wish you had been assigned to me, instead of this piece of crap!" as he looks over at me.

I am confused, I am befuddled, I am baffled, I am perplexed! I have never met this man before in my life. And yet he has some kind of issue and a certain disdain for me. He tells Firefighter Rod to go ahead and put his gear away while he has a word with me. Rod walks away, and Captain Dodd comes over to me as I stand barely inside the red door. And for two of the longest hours of my life, Captain Dodd recites to me how he didn't really want me, but since they sent me he has to take me. He quotes his short-term and long-term expectations. He mostly just repeats himself over and over in the tone and key of angry and with the breath of a dog that had licked his own butt. My legs are getting shaky from the standing, and my face is covered in dots of spittle from the frothy mouth of my new captain who obviously has no clue about the boundaries of personal space. Firefighter Rod placed his gear and left over an hour and a half ago.

As I listen to my new captain ramble on, all I can think of is to ask myself, "Is this all worth it? Do I really want to endure the crap that this man is going to give me every day?"

As I continue to nod and say, "Yes, sir" to everything Captain Dodd is pontificating, I have a flashback. I think back to the time when I was ten years old; I was playing in my front yard, when a boy from the neighborhood (the hood) came in my yard and threatened to beat me up. Well, the boy was the same age as me; the only difference was that boy was a big scary 11-year-old giant. He was six-foot-two and actually said cuss words, so I was afraid of him. I did what I thought was my best option--I jumped up and ran into the house! I burst through the front door and slammed it shut behind me. I turned and looked outside to see if he had followed me onto my porch.

When I realized that he had not followed me, my anxiety started to subside, until I looked out of the corner of my eye, and to my fright, my mother had been watching the entire incident from the living room window. She walked up to me with this monstrous look on her face and she said in a very unloving, non-motherly way, "Boy, this is your yard; don't you ever let somebody run you off of what belongs to you! Now you take your butt outside, and you run that boy out of your yard!"

So I walked back outside, scared but empowered. When that boy saw me back in my yard, he came over to me and asked me, "What are you doing back out here?"

I calmly explained, "My momma told me that I have to come out here and whoop your butt." Without any other warning, I commenced to do just that.

{LESSON 5} NO MATTER HOW BIG AND SCARRY THE BULLY IS IN YOUR LIFE, NEVER LET HIM RUN YOU OUT OF THE YARD THAT BELONGS TO YOU!

Somewhere in the latter part of the second hour of Captain Dodd's dissertation, I make up my mind that I have worked too hard and endured too much to let this guy run me out of my yard. Finally, God sends an angel to deliver me. Sergeant Mann interrupts forcefully, "Come on, Captain, give the boy a break! You have chewed him out for two hours and the boy isn't even on duty yet!"

Captain Dodd concedes and lets me go home. I never even have a chance to meet the other guys, nor to place my fire gear in a locker. I just put everything back in my car and drive home.

Three days later, I return for my first official day at Truck 8/Engine 10 Fire Station, and after my encounter with Captain Dodd, I am experiencing some anxiety, thinking of meeting the rest of my new firehouse family. I arrive nearly two hours before my shift is scheduled to start. Waiting for me at the front door is a very happy-faced firefighter who seems to be extremely eager to meet me. Firefighter Todd, a good-looking, smooth-talking ladies' man, introduces himself. He shows me to my locker, helps carry my gear, and gives me a quick tour of the station. I think, *Wow, this guy is more like it! He is really a great guy.* I ask Todd where everyone else is. He tells me that everyone is still sleep. The morning wake-up call doesn't sound until 0700 hours, and only the New Boy is up before 0700 Hours.

He continues, with his sneaky pretty-boy smile, "I was the New Boy, but as of this morning you are officially the New Boy." He then hands me a paper list that contains all of the New Boy chores, which must be finished upon arrival to duty every morning. The New Boy list:

1. Make sure the booster tank is filled with water (booster tank: the water tank on the fire truck that gives the initial supply of water to the fire hose)

2. Place the radio transceivers on the battery charger

3. Fill the water cooler that's on the fire truck with fresh drinking water and ice

4. Change the watch list (the list of company members names and assigned times for them to be awake, answering the phones and the doors)

5. Make fresh brewed coffee, tea, and Kool-Aid (2 full coffee cups of sugar per gallon pitcher)

6. Wash the dishes from the night before

7. Place the captain's gear on track

8. Fill out the roster card on the fire truck

9. Clean all of the sinks and toilets in the station

10. Mop every floor

Firefighter Todd apparently possessed these responsibilities for a full year. He had been looking forward to my arrival, expressly for the purpose of transferring those responsibilities to me. Todd graduated out of Fire Academy Class 169, a group not especially noted as being very bright, and certainly time would show the brilliance of my Recruit Class 170. We would prove to be the most exceptional Firefighter Recruit Class in the history of the Louisville Fire Department (of course, I may be a bit biased, and others may have some debate concerning this truth). Even though Todd just placed all of his work on my lap, I'm happy to have made his acquaintance. I can tell that he will be the fun part of my new family, and probably my new sibling rival.

As the morning dawns, shift change (shift change = the ending of one 24 hours and the beginning of a new 24 hours/ the arrival of the oncoming shift of firefighters and the relief and departure of duty of those firefighters who have served through the night) arrives. There are ten members of Platoon One preparing to leave, and ten members of platoon two arriving. This is the worst time of the day for a new member, because this is when the members can become like excited alligators working themselves into a frenzy because of some fresh meat, and in this case, I'm the freshest meat available. No one asks my name. It is as if I am wearing a name tag that reads "New Boy."

In many cases, firefighters can be crude, ornery, callous individuals. I think, after years of responding to every imaginable tragedy of life, the preferred mechanism for coping mentally is to laugh and joke about what you have seen and experienced, rather than actually express how you are feeling.

The first day goes by smoothly, and later in the afternoon, many of the guys are hanging around the apparatus floor grilling me with questions about what I learned in drill school. It's a firing squad of questions, and I'm not doing very well. But then, the bell rings loudly, and everyone jumps up in a hurry! It's not a fire alarm, it's the dinner bell. Nothing gets firefighters scurry faster than the call of "YO HO, IT'S TIME TO EAT!"

Everyone quickly lines up in the kitchen. Ten hungry men grab their plates and impatiently wait for their turn at the smorgasbord that has been expertly laid out in a row on the stove and the counter. Today is Friday, and that can only mean fried beer-battered Alaskan cod, firehouse baked beans with real country sausage embedded into every spoonful, baked macaroni and choke cheese (that's macaroni with so much cheddar cheese that it could choke you if it were not for the massive amount of farm butter to help it go down easy), twice-dipped fried potato wedges, sweet Kentucky Cole Slaw, and a small house salad (just so you can tell your wife that you were a good boy and had a salad for dinner).

As we all take our places at the table, eight blocks away there is a seven-year-old boy that just found his parents' cigarette lighter. This little boy takes the lighter into his bedroom where his three-year-old brother is already playing, and he shuts the door. He takes the lighter and flicks the switch to try and get the flame to come out like he has seen his parents do.

"Flick, Flick, Flame!" Wow, it works. Now he has the audience of his three-year-old brother. So he does it again, except this time he presses the lighter up against the flammable sheets on his bed. "Flick, Flick, Flick, Flame, and Whoosh!" The sheets quickly burst into flames and startle the boys backwards. As the seven-year-old drops the lighter, they both take off for the door with the seven-year-old in the lead. The seven-year-old bolts out of the bedroom, through the hallway and out the front door that leads into the front yard. A few minutes go by, and the bedroom begins to be totally engulfed in fire.

Meanwhile, in the back of the house, the parents are lounging on the couch in the TV room, completely oblivious to the inferno brewing in the front of their house; they have no smoke detectors installed. Eventually, the smoke and heat spread from the bedroom, through the hallway, and back to the TV room. Once the heat and smoke reach the parents. they are forced to retreat through the back door that leads to the back yard. Immediately they frantically begin the search for their two little boys. Hysterically, they cry out for anyone to help. "Somebody call the fire department!"

As I am into my last bite of gobbling down the remainder of my first fish sandwich, the fire knockout, tones and bells, ring out loudly. Dispatch announces, "Attention Engine 12, Telesqurt 23, Engine 10, Truck 8, and Battalion 3, Box alarm, report of a house fire with possible rescues."

Everyone drops their utensils and finishes their last chews of food as they race toward their side of the fire apparatus where their gear sits prepped for their arrival. I flip my shoes off and jump into my bunker pants and boots, simultaneously pulling my hood over my head; I grab my coat and jump into my seat. The huge bay doors are opened, the traffic light stops the oncoming vehicles, the truck pulls out, and the garage opener closes the bay doors behind us. This is all completed in less than thirty seconds.

As we start our response to the location, the dispatch repeats the information, but adds, "Attention all companies, we have multiple calls." This alerts the responding companies to the fact that this will probably be an actual fire and not a false alarm, because multiple callers are calling 911 to report the fire. As we approach, dispatch says that there are reports of two little boys trapped in the fire. The first fire company arrives on the scene two minutes after the initial dispatch, but it has been approximately six minutes since the blaze began. The battalion chief reports to all companies that a seven-year-old male is reported unharmed outside of the house, but there is a three-year-old boy that is unaccounted for.

By this time, the front of the house is overrun with bright orange fire and a thick black smoke. Engine 12 pulls up to the front of the house, and four firefighters jump off the apparatus and pull the Quick Line, 300ft of 1-3/4" pre-connected hose, and sprint toward the rear of the house. Two members of Truck 8 quickly get to the rear of the apparatus; they grab a "Quick Vent" chainsaw and pull off a 20-foot straight beam ladder and rush to the side of the burning house. They raise the ladder, start the chainsaw, and climb the ladder to the roof. They immediately begin the process of cutting a vent hole in the roof of the house (this is to release some of the super heat and smoke that is trapped inside the house, so that Engine 12 members can better fight the fire and find the possible victim). The two remaining members of Truck 8 grab axes, pry tools, plaster hooks for pulling ceilings, and an 8-foot A-frame room ladder, and head to the rear to make entry with the members of Engine 23. Members of Engine 23 stop at a hydrant down the street, allowing one member to get out and grab the yellow linen 5" hose and wrap it around the base of the hydrant, while the apparatus continues toward the front of the fire building to lay Engine 12 a water supply line. The member that is at the hydrant unwraps the hose and connects the hose coupling to the hydrant outlet. She then takes the hydrant wrench and places it on the operating nut at the top of the bonnet, turning the nut counter-clockwise to release the water flow. All of these firefighter movements are completed in a matter of less than two minutes.

When the members make entry through the rear of the house, they move quickly from room to room, making a search for the reported victim. They must feel their way through the black smoke that darkens every ray of sunlight, to the point of complete blindness. The members reach the little boys' bedroom. They crawl into the room on their hands and knees due to the heat of the fire banking down on them. They stay low to the ground and search near the window, over to the bed (feeling on the top and underneath the bed), and they finally circle back to a closet near the door of the room. You guessed it! When the boys took off running away from the initial burst of flames, the seven-year-old exited the room and out of the house, but the three-year-old went to his favorite hiding place; he hid in his bedroom closet and shut the door. When the firefighters find him, he has been roasting inside that closet for nearly seven minutes.

As he is being discovered, I am arriving on Engine 10. I am completely suited up, with my SCBA (self-contained breathing apparatus) strapped over my shoulders, and tools in both hands. My mind is set on battling the blaze. As I trot to the front of the house, Engine 12 members are running directly past me with this burnt baby in their arms. Everyone is in a frenzy to get this baby to the ambulance to receive treatment. I pause for a moment to process what I just saw, when I hear the Battalion Chief holler at me, "Ford, go jump on the ambulance and help them!"

Immediately I switch from firefighter mode to EMT mode (Emergency Medical Technician). I drop my tools, pull off my helmet, SCBA, face piece, and coat and scurry to the ambulance. When I open the side door of the ambulance, there he is: a small, chubby, white three-year-old baby boy who is charcoal-black from the scorching of the heat in his bedroom that penetrated through the door of his favorite hiding place. My heart sinks into the pit of my stomach. The boy is alive and conscious, and his eyelids are burnt off, so he stares up at me silently. He is unable to speak, scream, or squish his face in pain, because his skin has tightened and constricted any facial movement.

The paramedic declares loudly, "This boy is as good as dead!"

I don't know this paramedic, and I assume that he is just overwhelmed by the moment of this responsibility of saving the boy's life. I shout angrily back at him, pointing my finger in his face, "Shut your mouth--this boy is alive, and he can hear you, and you are not God to declare that this boy is dead!"

I turn my attention back to the boy; placing some medical gloves on my hands, I reach to touch him, but he is so hot the gloves nearly melt. I find the bottom of his foot isn't scorched, so I touch him there and I begin to pray. Everyone gets quiet.

As tears stream down my face, I simply pray, "Dear God, help this little boy; he really needs you now, and if possible don't let him die, for the sake of his mother and father who love him. Amen."

As we speed with lights and sirens to the hospital, we do all that we can. The emergency room team is waiting for us as we pull up to the hospital. We roll him in on the stretcher and the doctors and nurses grab the sheets with him lying on them and transfer him to one of their hospital beds. Just like that, he is gone, and I will never physically see that little boy again. One would think that's the close of this incident. Unfortunately, I would never stop seeing that burnt little boy in my mind for the next twenty years.

That 24-hour shift couldn't end fast enough. I need to get home. When I arrive home, I am merrily greeted by my three-year-old and seven-year-old daughter and son. After looking tragedy in the face, I need to see that my children are safe.

From the day of that fire, when I return back to the fire station, till today, no one ever speaks about the pain and trauma that we all suffered seeing that little boy. At the time, firefighter culture is that everyone has to play the tough guy, and not expose the fact that you are stressed, hurt, traumatized, overwhelmed, emotionally compromised. Today, fire departments around the world recognize and treat the needs of the firefighter's mental and emotional health.

For the record, I saw that same paramedic a few months later and he informed me that the burned little boy was still alive. That was the last word I ever heard concerning that little boy. I pray that he is alive and doing well.

CHAPTER 6
Final Moments

How many times have you rushed out of your house without offering a warm hug or a sweet kiss to your significant other, or sent your children off to school or ball practice with no thought in mind that this might be the last time, the last chance for some meaningful exchange or embrace? As firefighters, you learn very quickly just how fragile life is, and how one unexpected moment can change your world forever.

It's Saturday morning "scrub-out" day at Engine 10/Truck 8 Fire Station. Scrub-out day is the day that firefighters open the bay doors and pull out all of the fire engines and trucks onto the front ramp. This is so that the entire apparatus floor is completely uncovered. Once this is done, the floor is sprinkled with massive amounts of Spic-'n'-Span soap or some cleansing powder. The garden hose is then brought into the bay, where water is sprinkled all over the floor. Then everyone grabs a deck brush and begins to scrub the floors (everyone except for the captain and the cook). This tradition of scrubbing the apparatus floor goes back nearly one hundred years.

[5]It began as early as the mid-1800s, when fire horses where introduced to the community service of fighting fires. As the equipment for fighting fires became to heavy for mere men to carry and transport, horses were introduced. Several new inventions in the 1800s, such as the street box alarm and the sliding pole, enhanced firefighters' ability to respond to the scene of a fire more quickly.

In the 1800s, there was no greater addition to firefighter response than the introduction of fire horses. The fire horses were kept in horse stalls directly behind the fire station or kept inside the fire station on the first floor (or sometimes called the apparatus floor) underneath the second or third floors where the firefighters lived and slept. When the fire bell rang or the alarm sounded, the stall doors would open automatically, and the horses would react by running out and positioning themselves into their assigned places in front of the steam wagons. The driver would pull a rope, and the horse hitches, collars, and harness that were suspended overhead would be released to sit down on the backs of these trained horses. A firefighter would then tie the harness belts around the horses' necks. The signal to proceed would be given, and like a flash of lightning, the horses would charge toward the fire scene, pulling tools, large extension ladders, hoses, pipes, steam engines, and as many as twenty firefighters. The horses were usually harnessed and out of the door responding to the fire incidents in less than thirty seconds.

These glorious chariots and horses revolutionized the fire service and saved countless lives. That was the good part. The other side to this coin is that you actually had a 1,500-pound saddle-bred or Thoroughbred horse living in the same house,

---

5   (Aurora Regional Fire Museum , 2009)

underneath the floor you ate and slept on. You can only imagine the strong fragrance permeating from the first floor all the way to your living quarters, especially on those hot summer days. So this is why the weekly scrub-out was introduced, so that the fresh stains of the horses' escaped rear product that hit the floor could be washed away. That is why even a hundred years later, firefighters carry on the tradition of scrub-out. Fortunately, nowadays we only have to scrub away oil stains from the trucks and some small debris.

This Saturday morning, it's bright and warm outside, which causes everyone to be a bit playful and very careless with the water hose. Everyone seems to be getting "accidentally" sprayed by the water. Bummmmm!!!! The alarm sounds. Everyone goes silent. The radio reports loudly, "Attention Engine 10, make a BLS (Basic Life Support) incident, a pedestrian struck--a pick-up truck versus a pedestrian."

The location is given, and a report that there may be some children involved is also presented. Captain Bers tells Firefighter Coop to stay back and continue cooking breakfast. Firefighter Bernie from Truck 8 takes Coop's place on the engine. As we are traveling toward the scene of the accident, I place my medical gloves on and sit back and think about all the possible treatment options that I may need to deploy on this accident scene. It just so happens that I am the only Emergency Medical Technician (EMT) on the engine today, so the captain may need to lean on my expertise.

Upon arriving on the scene, in my first snapshot look, I see a parked car in front of a residential house, with a little two-year-old girl sitting in her car seat. There is a pickup truck sitting in the middle of the street; it also has a little two-year-old girl sitting in her car seat. There is a tall man in a flannel shirt standing between the truck in the street and the parked vehicle. He is holding both sides of his face, tears in his eyes, and he is obviously extremely distressed. I am briefly confused by what I'm seeing, until we see the final piece to this puzzle. There he is, the driver of the parked vehicle, lying underneath the front bumper of the pick-up truck. Apparently, the victim was out early Saturday morning with his little daughter, taking care of some errands. He just arrived back home and completed parking the vehicle directly in front of his house. He stepped outside of the vehicle and proceeded to retrieve his daughter from her car seat. He opened the driver's side rear door, which also happened to be on the street side instead of the sidewalk side.

At the same time, the man in the flannel shirt, driving the pick-up truck, was driving down this same quiet neighborhood street with his two-year-old daughter strapped safely in her car seat, when she started crying; figuring she probably needed her sippy cup, he attempted to turn his body a little toward the right rear of the vehicle and hand her the cup. As he did this, without him realizing, he was actually now veering the entire truck to the right and smashed forcefully into the the man in the street unbuckling his daughter. The man in the pickup truck slammed on the brakes, but it was too late; the irrevocable damage was done. The victim was carried a few feet on top of the pickup truck's front bumper until it came to a sudden stop. The tall man in the flannel shirt quickly jumped out of his truck to investigate, but the victim was surely killed instantly.

There wasn't anything of significance that we could do to help the victim, seeing that he was already dead. As we were waiting on the police to arrive and conduct a vehicular homicide investigation, my mind took a mental picture of all the irony in this tragic scene. First, the stunned and bewildered look on the face of the man in the flannel shirt from the pickup truck as he clutches his daughter tightly. He has to be wishing he could go back in time and change the final moments before he decided to take his eyes off the road and turning to hand his crying daughter a sippy cup, knowing that in his careless actions, he just killed a man, and that using a sippy cup to keep his two-year-old daughter from some temporary tears cost another man's two-year-old daughter a lifetime of tears and the absence of her father's arms to hold and comfort her.

Secondly, this dead man stretched out in the street...surely when he woke up this morning and as he left his home, he had no thought that this would be his last day alive. This dead man, as he returned to the safety of his home, and pulled directly in front of his house, on this quiet secluded street, and as he parked his vehicle, absolutely did not imagine nor consider that this would be his final moment. He could not have known, that the moment he got out of his vehicle and reached for the handle, and peered into the vehicle at his two-year-old's smiling face, that he would be seeing his daughter for the last time, and that she would be seeing him alive for the last time.

The lessons that I have learned in this incident are so relevant for us today. This wasn't some freak accident, but an every-hour occurrence. In the United States, nearly 500,000 people are injured or killed every year due to distracted drivers. In my twenty-three years as a firefighter I have seen drivers texting, holding babies, holding dogs, putting on make-up--I once seen a woman eating a bowl of milk and cereal with a spoon as she drove down the highway. Come on, people; let's do better, let's be more conscientious in our driving habits, so that we will not be the cause of someone's, or our own, "Final Moment."

{LESSON 6} "Let's be more conscientious in our driving habits, so that we will not be the cause of someone's, or our own "Final Moment."

As a new member of the fire company, Saturday mornings were always a day to look forward to at the firehouse. Yes, I still had my New Boy chores; I still was the low man, I still had to spend eight hours studying my probationary book; yes, I still had to clean five toilets. But the Saturday-morning difference was the smell that permeated throughout the station as I conducted my morning routine. I know that I have informed you about my wife's so called "Fire Department smell," but there is another firehouse smell. It's the smell of waffles and pancakes sizzling on the griddle in Crisco fat or salted butter. It's the smell of eight pounds of oven- roasted, crispy bacon, laid out on four large cookie sheets. It's the smell of three dozen homemade buttermilk biscuits, with liquid butter brushed all over, rising and browning to a flakey, golden perfection. It's the smell of fresh sliced green granny apples, basting in a caldron of butter, cinnamon, and brown sugar. It's the smell of thick-cut Idaho potatoes, freshly carved onions, with a generous spread of seasoning salt and pepper sautéed and lightly frying in a large uncovered iron skillet. It's the smell of three dozen eggs, scrambled and poured into a skillet, with diced red and green peppers. It's the smell of white sausage gravy packed with four pounds of chopped country sausage, flavored with a hint of real maple syrup. Yes, on Saturday mornings, the firehouse smells like Bob Evan's, Waffle House, Cracker Barrel, and IHOP all wrapped up in one.

The cook reaches for the intercom, taps the mic with his finger three times, and begins to say, "Yo ho, it's time to eat- -come and get it!!" Before he can finish his statement, I've sprinted into the kitchen, grabbed my plate, and I'm standing there next to the prepared food, in second place, waiting only for the cook to take his rightful place as first partaker. As the other guys file in, the battalion chief goes ahead of me, then the two captains both jump in front of me, then the two sergeants, and finally one of the older guys uses the back of his plastic plate to gently pop me on the back of my head and says, "Hey, New Boy, get to the back of the line!"

Crap! I think, *I don't want to wait for these eleven large hungry men to go through this smorgasbord before me!* Have you ever been starving on a Friday night, so you and your friends drive to your favorite restaurant? When you enter, you see fifty people sitting in the waiting area, and the hostess informs you that you have at least a one-hour wait, and she hands you the dreaded buzzer. This is how I feel, standing there salivating, and trying not to look infuriated and agitated that they are taking so long. Well, after half of eternity passed, I'm finally back where I started originally (second place). Nine guys have already poured their freshly squeezed orange juice and have sat down to eat. It's finally my turn. I grab two biscuits and open them both up and smother them with at least a cup of that white sausage gravy. I pull off four strips of that crispy bacon, but three more slices seem to be connected and attached to the other strips (I don't bother to disconnect them). As I am reaching for the spatula, to scrape up the crispiest parts of the fried potatoes and onions, the unthinkable happens.

Buummmm!!!! Buummmmmm!!!! The knockout system rings out loudly. "NOOOOOO!!" I scream within myself. I stuff a piece of bacon in my mouth, slam my plastic plate down, and race toward the fire truck. It's a medical incident, being reported as a sixty-year-old male unresponsive. The Engine 10 crew unenthusiastically leave the kitchen and mount up on the fire truck. We are out of the fire station in less than sixty seconds. As we arrive on the scene (to the residence) the ambulance crew pulls up to the house at the same time. The medical crew happen to have an extra paramedic, who is in training. Six of us now enter the house, where the door had been purposely left open for our access. The wife urgently walks into the living room and motions for us to come into the dining area. As we come into the dining room we notice a very neat room and a neatly arranged table setting, with a man sitting, but slumped over the table. The sergeant and the captain quickly grab the man under both his arms and both of his legs, placing him supine (flat on his back) on to the floor. One of the EMTs checks for a carotid pulse (that's the pulse in the neck) and finds none. While the paramedic hooks the patient to the heart monitor, two of the other medics begin CPR (Cardiopulmonary Resuscitation) on the patient.

I go back to the front door in order to pull the stretcher in from off of the front porch. When I return, I can see that the man's wife has left the dining room and gone and sat on her bed in the room down the hall. She isn't screaming, she isn't crying; she just has a strange blank look on her face as she stares up at the ceiling. She is in the room next to where we are working, so I leave the stretcher there with the team and I walk gently into the woman's bedroom. I kneel down next to the bed and facing her, and I ask if she is alright.

She turns toward me and says with a slow bewilderment, "I just walked into the kitchen to get him some sugar."

I stare back at her, with my bewildered look, to let her know that I don't understand what she just said. So she recaps what just happened. She says, "We woke up this morning, and he sat at the table waiting for some tea, like he does every Saturday morning. I brought the tea to the table and sat down at the table with him. We talked for a few minutes, and I noticed that there was no sugar on the table. So I got up from the table, walked into the kitchen, reached into the cabinet for the sugar, and walked back into the room and he was gone. He was just gone." She stares back up to the ceiling and continues, "I couldn't have been gone for more than two minutes, and he was gone." She looks back at me, "We have been together for over forty-five years, and now he's gone. What am I supposed to do now?"

As we sit there, I am really hopeful that there will be some good news from the other room; maybe the team performing CPR will be successful in reviving her husband. But they are not; he is dead.

Over the years when I think about what can happen in a day, I always think about this lady and the bewildered look on her face, and the quiet distress that she displayed as she pondered the unexpected final moments, that she had experienced with the man that she had loved since she was a teenager. [6]My favorite book says, *"No one knows what will happen tomorrow. For what is life? It is only a vapor that appears for a little time and then vanishes away."*

I wish I could become more skilled in conveying this message to every spouse, every parent, every friend. I know you have heard the saying "Here today and gone tomorrow," but as this woman learned, "Here one minute and gone the next." We must all remember to value and savor each moment with our loved ones, because the next moment isn't guaranteed.

> *{Lesson 7} "Spend affectionate time and take full advantage of each day with your loved ones, because life is only a vapor that appears for a little time and then vanishes away."*

A few years ago, I was sent to work at a LFD fire station in the south end of town to be the apparatus operator for the day. We received a report that there was an explosion in a residential area. Now over my twenty-three years of service, I have responded to the aftermath of a number of explosions, including a gas line rupture that completely reduced a two-story house into a large pile of wooden sticks. So, I am imagining the worst. But as we arrive on the scene, this one is a bit more unusual. There is a young lady lying in the front yard, with her clothes almost completely burnt off her body. Three of her neighbors are already standing over her to provide some assistance, but her body is lifeless. I glance over at the house to try to piece together what has happened. The house has been nearly blown completely off its foundation, but it is entirely intact. Apparently, the young lady was remodeling

---

6   (Bible)

the house, for her and her fiancé to soon move into. She was preparing the basement floors using a type of polyurethane. Unfortunately, she failed to provide any ventilation, nor did she understand the need to turn the gas pilot lights off, and any electrical sources to prevent explosions. The explosive force was so powerful, we can't immediately discern whether she was blown out of the basement from underneath the frame of the structure, or whether she was blown out of one of the windows.

The EMS crew arrives, and with the assistance of the fire-fighters, quickly places a C-Collar around her neck for stabilization, slides a back board underneath her body, and loads her onto the stretcher, and into the ambulance. By the time she is placed into the ambulance, she is already dead. A few minutes pass, and a car recklessly pulls up in front of the house. A distressed young man bolts from the vehicle; glancing at the house that is sitting off its foundation, he runs directly to the ambulance. As the young man reaches the back doors of the ambulance, the fire personnel grab him as if we are the Secret Service.

"Who are you?" we ask the man.

He screams in one breath, "I am her fiancé, is she alright!!"

One of us explains, "She is not alright."

We slowly open the doors to allow him access, but when he steps in and sees her naked, burned, lifeless body, he seemed to instantly lose all the strength in his body, and he collapses to the floor. We watch him as he goes through a long range of emotions, which is quite understandable. Once he regains his strength and he steps out of the ambulance, I bring him over to the steps of the house to sit with me, so that I can get some information about the victim and the house. Then he displays an emotion that is surprising to me--guilt! He explains how he and his fiancée were scheduled to get married in a few weeks, and how they have been working to prep this old house that they recently purchased. But two days ago they got into an argument about something really small and stupid, and he threatened to call the wedding off. So he spent the past few days away from the house. That's why she was down in the basement working on the floors by herself.

Wow, I am speechless. I mean not only has this man just found the love of his life traumatically killed, he has to live with the fact that he may have been able to prevent it if he had been present. But more distressing to me would be the fact that the "Final Moments" that he spent with her were wasted on some trivial, insignificant, petty argument with mean words spoken that can never be taken back. This is a story of a couple with a tragic ending that should have never happened. My favorite book encourages the readers, [7]*"Don't let the sun go down while you are still angry."* Many times, we allow petty differences or small offences to cause division or separation between us and those we love. I hope the final moments that I spend with my wife, my children, my parents, my siblings, my friends will be filled with hugs and kisses and the powerfully sweet words of "I LOVE YOU."

{LESSON 8} "Stop wasting precious moments being angry or bitter with your loved ones."

---

7   (Paul)

58

CHAPTER 7
Firefighter Comedy

There are very few, if any careers that offer the employee such a rare and diversified opportunity to perform work that possesses such immense purpose, boundless excitement, imminent danger, remarkable responsibility, heartbreaking tragedy, splendidly close friendships, and a sense of belonging to something--some cause greater than yourself. Because of the uniqueness of the firefighter life and the tragic nature of the incidents that the firefighter encounters, there has evolved a very distinct coping mechanism that supports the firefighter's overall mental health. Laughter is the coping mechanism that best soothes, heals, and recalibrates the firefighter's mind from these tragic life events that they experience on a daily basis. Now before I move on to share with you some additional stories, allow me to first warn you about something that you may not know about firefighters unless you have had the privilege (or misfortune) of being somehow connected to one. Firefighters can be some of the most mature, professional, sensitive, discreet, politically correct individuals that you will ever encounter, while on an emergency scene or in the view of the public. But behind closed doors, and generally away from public view, they can soon become some of the most playful, immature, insensitive, nonpolitically correct, vulgar, mischievous individuals that one could ever meet. We beg your forgiveness in advance!

{WARNING} "In general, firefighters have a warped, sometimes twisted, often inappropriate and non-politically correct sense of humor. We beg your forgiveness in advance."

From my very first day of working at the fire station, I noticed that there was always an abundance of laughter and plenty of mischievous amusement that was an everyday, all-day occurrence. In many ways, there is a distinct culture of playful camaraderie. In the beginning, it has the tendency to catch you by surprise, especially since, as the newest addition to the firehouse family, you are unfortunately the focus and main recipient of this playful attention. It is easy to misinterpret this until you are fully integrated into the culture.

One of my favorite LFD comedians is a guy that we affectionately nicknamed Ricky Bobby; he is one of the sneakiest, most playful jokesters in the department. One of the reasons that his playful pranks have been so successful is due to the fact that he is one of the most serious, professional, well-respected officers in the department. Consequently, if you didn't actually know him, you would never suspect that he is the one who pranked you. Ricky Bobby describes best the difference between fire department comedy and what is funny and acceptable comedy to normal/sane, reasonable people, with a story that he tells about an incident with his wife.

One particular weekend that he was off from work, he was

driving his wife, and twelve- and ten-year-old sons to a lake area out in a rural section of beautiful Bluegrass Kentucky. After driving for a few hours, they decided to stop at an old country general store to refresh themselves. You know, the old store with the old rickety porch that you step onto to enter, and the wood floor that taps with sound with your every step; and there are glass showcases with all sorts of baked goods, trinkets, and souvenirs--the kind of store that makes you want to grab one of those cold bottles of orange soda pop and go sit in one of those rocking chairs on the front porch.

Well, after they all had refreshed themselves, each of them stepped in line with the snack that they chose for the road. As they waited for their turn with the cashier, the wife couldn't help noticing the jars of candy, which surely reminded her of the childhood candy that she loved so much. So she scooped out a handful of the very colorful gumballs. When Ricky Bobby saw his wife with a handful of round colorful gumballs, his firehouse comedic instinct kicked in! So, he set his wife up for the comic routine.

He said, "Hey Babe, what kind of candy is that in your hand?" and because she is a normal, mature, reasonable forty-year-old woman, she didn't see the prank coming.

"Gumballs," she revealed innocently, as she opened her palm wide, to show him. And without thought or hesitation, Ricky Bobby swiftly slapped the bottom of her hand with a forceful upward motion, which caused every gumball that she was holding to fly into the air in thirty different directions! Ricky Bobby watched with great delight and a fantastic grin on his face as the blue, red, orange, white, and green gum-balls floated in the air like fireworks in a night sky. But as the gumballs crashed against the wooden floor, drawing everyone's attention, he instantly noticed the look on his wife's face. You know that look that your mom gave you after you just showed her your bad report card, or some note from the teacher that reported your bad behavior in class. Yeah, that was the look he was receiving from his wife, and everyone else in the store.

Everyone in the store stared in amazement at his stupidity, including the boys, who looked at Dad with a very bewildered look as if to say, "Wow, Dad, that was childish."

His wife simply said to him as she glared at him with disappointed eyes, "You're an idiot."

Realizing the trouble that he was now in, he quickly responded, "You're right, Babe, I am an idiot."

As he dived onto the floor to pick up the scattered gumballs, he was thinking, *Man, that joke kills at the firehouse--I mean, that prank is a fire department classic! It never gets old.* To this day, if you perform this prank perfectly at the firehouse in front of everyone, there is immediate laughter, and everyone will be further entertained by the significant chase that will ensue by the victim and the wrestling match that will commence upon the victim catching the culprit. It's serious big fun! That's why I say that you can't fully appreciate the firehouse comedy until you come to understand the firehouse culture.

Firehouse comedy is a concoction of slapstick, buffoon-ery, clowning, foolery, hijinks, horsing around, monkey busi-ness, roughhousing, shenanigans, and simple or elaborately planned pranks, mingled with a heavy measure of storytelling and tall tales. The firehouse comedy is rarely mean-spirited or meant to cause a person harm. Of course, I am indoctrinated into this culture from day one. It really is harmless jokes on my first night; my captain requests a pair of wire pliers from me on a motor vehicle accident to disconnect a car battery. As he holds his hand out in anticipation of me pulling the pli-ers out of my fire coat pocket, what I actually pull out is a red and white baby rattle that someone stuck in my pocket. So of course my captain looks at me with stern angry eyes, as if I have exchanged my pliers for a red and white baby rattle.

Then again, after speaking with some of my classmates who explain to me about their first nights, I actually think that my experience is easy and light-hearted. One of my young, innocent friends told me that he had finished all of his firehouse nightly chores, and he thought he was the last person to enter the bedroom. He made his way to his twin-sized bed, got in, and pulled the covers up to his chin (he wasn't used to the cold temperature that every firehouse bedroom maintains). As he lay there for about a minute, trying to get acclimated to his new surroundings, the bedroom door opened, and to his shock a butt-naked firefighter stood in the light of the doorway. He really didn't like what he saw, but he couldn't turn his eyes away from the strange sight of a naked man standing in the light of the doorway! He thought, *This can't be good.* Finally, and unfortunately, the naked man started coming over toward my friend's bed.

When he arrived, he said, "Hey, New Boy, I know this is your first time being away from home, and I normally spend the first night with every New Boy, just to comfort him during his first night, so that he doesn't feel lonely and miss his Mommy. So scoot over and let me under those covers."

Of course, my buddy could hear the rest of the firefighters laughing in their beds. Now when my friend gets to this part in the story, he always says he jumped out of the bed and ran away, and that's the end of the story. But when I hear this from other firefighters, they of course embellish the story by saying that all they saw was the old naked firefighter get under the covers; they don't remember anyone running away. Now, me being a firefighter fully brainwashed in the firehouse comedy club, I always reply back to my friend that I don't really know who to believe--I mean, who can say what really happened in a dark bedroom?

When it comes to firehouse humor, there really isn't

anything or any topic that's off limits. Not your mother, father, brothers, sisters, wife, nor religion. There is nothing too sacred. I'm remembering my first year at Engine 10/Truck 8 fire station. The year 1995, I had set out on a spiritual journey, and had informed my captain that I would be fasting every Tuesday and Wednesday until 4:00 p.m. This went on for nearly a year; I would skip the firehouse breakfast or lunch and at 4:00 in the afternoon, I would come into the kitchen and grab a snack to hold me over until dinnertime. To be honest, I had been quite surprised at how understanding and considerate the guys had been to me during this spiritual journey that I was on.

One Wednesday afternoon I was kind of pacing the floor; for some reason, I was particularly hungry that day. I left out of the Joker room to go into the kitchen to check the clock and see what time it was (Joker room = the room with the house radio, fire phone, and watch list). I didn't wear a watch, and this was before most people carried a cell phone. I walked into the kitchen, as I normally did, to view the clock. I thought, *Yes! Its 4:00 already!* I immediately broke into the refrigerator and built me a big, sloppy crunchy peanut butter and strawberry jelly sandwich. As I took my second messy bite, with strawberry jelly sliding down the right side of my mouth, I had a funny feeling that I was being watched. I looked up to see all of the guys slowly trickle in with big fat grins on their faces. I wasn't sure what the meaning of this was; I just understood that it couldn't be good for me.

The senior firefighter, Chuck, spoke first. "Ford, Ford, Ford...whatcha, doing New Boy?"

With my mouth full and still slowly chewing, "Eat'n," I replied.

By this time, there were seven men standing around me. "Ford, I thought you wasn't supposed to be eat'n until 4:00," Chuck mumbled, looking down at me with a cigarette sticking out of his mouth.

So I looked up at the clock and it read 4:10 p.m. Then, I realized what was going on. These sneaky scumbags had taken notice of the fact that I didn't wear a watch, and had been watching my tendency to come into the kitchen to check the clock on the wall for the time. These knuckleheads turned the clock hour hand back one hour! It was really only 3:10 PM. SMH (shaking my head)! Again, for firefighters there are very few things that are off limits; there is virtually nothing sacred.

Take for instance, the incident Engine Company10 responds to, one early afternoon. We pull into a nice, quiet neighborhood on the southern edge of Louisville, and up to a small ranch-style home. The dispatch has informed us that this will be an elderly woman found nonresponsive by family members. As we enter the tiny house, the four family members meet us at the living room door. They are emotional. They are sobbing softly. They explain that their mother is in the other room, and they don't believe she's alive. Captain Bers and I step into the room and find the elderly female lying on the bedroom floor. I kneel down next to the woman and find her hard and cold to the touch; rigor mortis has set in. I attempt to find a carotid pulse in the woman's neck; there is none. At this point in my fire department career, I have been on the department nearly three years, enough time for Captain Bers to trust my judgment, but he still kneels down and feels her neck for a possible pulse. He concurs with me that there's no pulse. Normally, the lack of a pulse would send us right into

CPR operations, but due to the woman's body being cold and stiff, we decide there isn't any use for CPR.

Captain Bers walks out of the room to give the family the unfortunate news that they have already assumed. "I'm sorry, but she has most certainly passed. There isn't anything we can do for her."

The family bursts with emotion, weeping and wailing as they embrace each other. Captain Bers just stands there in the midst of the sadness of the moment. He finally breaks the silence when he places the brick-shaped transceiver radio to his mouth and cancels the ambulance, and calls for Dispatch to send the coroner. I never leave the side of the deceased elderly woman; I feel like she was still my patient until I have been relieved by someone. Captain Bers comes into the bedroom and stands next to where I am kneeling; the only thing to do is wait. Nearly twenty minutes pass by when finally, the coroner walks through the front door. He is a man in is late fifties, short and kind of pudgy. His voice is loud and his demeanor is of a man that has walked in amongst a group of his friends.

In his big voice he says, "Good afternoon, everybody! So what's going on here? Who am I here to see?" Mr. Coroner ruins the ambience of mourning and stuns all of us in the process. The family doesn't say a word; they just point him into the bedroom where we are. Mr. Coroner walks in with a smile on his face, shuts the bedroom door, and says, "Good afternoon, fellas." He places his black equipment bag onto the bed and pulls out his stethoscope. He comes over and kneels next to the deceased elderly woman. He places the stethoscope on the woman's chest to ensure the absence of a heartbeat, before he can officially declare the woman to be dead.

Captain Bers and I watch as the coroner's facial expression quickly transitions from a smile to a look of intense distress. We both perk up with concern, but what could it be? It's a deceased person. The coroner moves the stethoscope to the woman's neck, and immediately turns to us and says emphatically, "This woman is alive!"

My eyes pop out of their sockets, Cap's tongue smacks the floor, and both of our hearts stop beating! I mean, we have let this lady lie here for over twenty minutes without providing her with any medical care! Not to mention, we told her family that she was dead! Seconds of silence pass, but Mr. Coroner can no longer contain his straight face, he erupts with laughter, saying, "Look at you boys' faces! Boy's she's good and dead!"

We aren't saying anything; we are in complete shock. Now I know why he shut the bedroom door when he came into the room. He was planning this from the moment that he walked in.

Remember, "In general, firefighters have a warped, sometimes twisted, often times inappropriate and non-politically correct sense of humor." Apparently, this also applies to coroners! I guess we deserve this, but I still feel like smacking that silly smirk off this old man's face. Captain Bers, who has a reputation for being short-tempered, looks as if he is about to explode. Instead, he looks at the man with a very nasty look, and just says to me, "Ford, let's go!"

I have come to understand and appreciate the warped sense of humor that is so prevalent in the fire and emergency services professions. Over the past twenty-three years of my fire service, I have certainly had moments of stress, distress, and experienced emotional trauma because of the tragedy and traumatic life and death situations of others. I had not recognized it in those moments, but I certainly realize now, that the support that was most helpful after a traumatic incident was returning to the fire station and not having time to dwell on the negative, because someone in the house would lighten the mood and energize the atmosphere with some prank or joke induced laughter. The joke may have been crude and inappropriate for public audiences, but the laughter that it produced brought some temporary healing to the stress and emotional trauma that each firefighter was experiencing.

{LESSON 9} *"Laughter is God's catch-all medicine, capable of providing mental, emotional, and physical healing."*

According to mental health specialist [8]Dr. Jeanne Segal:

Laughter relaxes the whole body. A good, hearty laugh relieves physical tension and stress, leaving your muscles relaxed for up to forty-five minutes after.

Laughter boosts the immune system. Laughter decreases stress hormones and increases immune cells and infection-fighting antibodies, thus improving your resistance to disease.

Laughter triggers the release of endorphins, the body's natural feel-good chemicals. Endorphins promote an overall sense of well-being and can even temporarily relieve pain.

Laughter protects the heart. Laughter improves the function of blood vessels and increases blood flow, which can help

---

8   (Jeanne Segal, 2017)

protect you against a heart attack and other cardiovascular problems.

Laughter stops distressing emotions. You can't feel anxious, angry, or sad when you're laughing.

Laughter helps you relax and recharge. It reduces stress and increases energy, enabling you to stay focused and accomplish more.

Laughter shifts perspective, allowing you to see situations in a more realistic, less threatening light. A humorous perspective creates psychological distance, which can help you avoid feeling overwhelmed and diffuse conflict.

Laughter draws you closer to others, which can have a profound effect on all aspects of your mental and emotional health.

CHAPTER 8
Gun Fires

Like many of the great fire departments in this country and around the world, the Louisville Fire Department is what is called an all-hazards department. This simply means that we train our members to respond to numerous types of emergency incidents. For the Louisville Fire Department, this includes: high angle rescue, hazardous materials response, confined space rescue, trench rescue, building collapse rescue, fire extinguishment, emergency medical service, motor vehicle extrication, dive rescue, swift water rescue, and most recently, active aggressor/active shooter rescue task force. When most people think about their local fire personnel, they think about them responding to and being responsible for fighting fires in their community. Of course they would think that way, we are called "firefighters." But what most people really never understand is how often we respond to incidents where the fire is that of one that explodes from the barrel of a gun.

Midway through my first year on the department, the Engine 10 crew and I respond to the report of gunfire in a residential area. This incident is before the department established the scene safety protocols that we have today, which mandate fire personnel to stage in a secure area until local police can secure the scene. So as we arrive to what is usually a very quiet and uneventful neighborhood in our first alarm district, a woman emerges from the back yard of the residence. She frantically motions for us to come to the back yard. But just as we grab our gear and the medical kit, she angrily declares, "I didn't call for the fire department, I called for an ambulance!"

Captain Dodd, without breaking stride, quickly explains to her that we are trained medical emergency responders, and the ambulance is on the way. "Tell us what has happened!" Captain Dodd forcefully demands. Before she can say a word, we see a man laid out flat on his back, on a concrete pad, next to the garage in the rear of the back yard.

The woman begins to explain, "I was in the house, my husband walked outside, and a few minutes later I heard a gun fire. I looked out the window and he was lying on the ground!"

Engine 10 Crew begins to provide the man with some medical attention. The man's gun is sitting next to him. We wouldn't require Sherlock Holmes to figure this one out. This man has tried to commit suicide. I say tried, because he had obviously pointed the gun to the left side of his head but had apparently flinched as he pulled the trigger. This caused the bullet to enter more of the front part of the left side of his head. This is also the reason why it did not provide him with immediate death. This is the first time I have ever seen a person shot. It isn't what I imagined in my mind, nor what I have seen in the movies. There is very little blood--just a small entrance hole on the side of the man's head, and a small exit hole in the front of the man's head.

As we attend to this man, the fire personnel understand that there is nothing of consequence that we can do for him; his death is imminent. Nearly two minutes after our arrival, a group of teenaged boys with basketballs in their hands approach the back yard from the alley. They cautiously approach the yard at first, but then one of the boys screams out, "Dad!" He rushes over to his dad's lifeless body and with an emotion that can only be described as "angry love," he shouts at his dad, "No, no--why, why you do that!"

The teenaged boy begins to reach for his dad; I can't tell if it is to give him a loving embrace or to grab him to try and shake some sense into him. Sergeant Kay gently clutches the boy's arm and pulls him back. The boy's friends are standing in the alley, and by this time a few more bystanders have joined them. I watch the boy move from "angry love" to embarrassment that people are watching. His emotional outburst turns its focus onto the bystanders; he screams at them with a flurry of curse words, telling them to go away and to stop looking at his dad.

Something strange happens to me in this moment as I'm attempting to provide care to this patient. I realize that I don't like him. I know that I don't really know him, but I too am angry with this man. The wife's panicked, white, ghost-faced expression as she paces anxiously around us, as if somewhat hopeful that we would be able to perform some miracle, and the teenaged son's "angry love" turned to embarrassment, have somehow been transferred to me. In some way I begin to identify with their agony and distress.

I think, *Why did he do this, what could be so bad in life that he should take his own?* As far as I can tell, he lives in a nice neighborhood, has a nice house, and he apparently has a wife and son that love him. Why would he do this to his wife and son, and why did he do it in some place so open, where his son's friends and the neighbors could see, and cause his family this hurt and embarrassment? A wife needs her husband, and a teenaged son certainly needs his father! In the middle of a bright sunny summer day, he decides to fire a bullet into his head and leave his family without a warning or a goodbye, and leave them wondering why? I simply don't understand this madness!

The paramedics arrive on the scene, hook him to the EKG monitor, and ultimately declare the man dead. Engine 10 crew packs up our equipment, and in a few moments this incident for us is over. Just like the next few thousand incidents that I respond to and exit from, I know I will never see these people again. They will become a distant memory. But because I feel such a tremendous emotional transfer from the wife and son, they are some of the people that I can never quite shake from my mind. Also, I am left to ponder the incomplete story of this man, this husband and father who thought so little of his life that he would end it on that summer afternoon in his back yard. I walk away with disdain for this selfish coward of a man, who considered only his pain, over the lifetime of pain that he would cause his family.

This incident happens in the early 1990s, when there is very little exposure given to men's mental health issues. In my ignorance, I do not understand the significant impact that suicide is having in the United States. [9]According to the CDC,

---

9   (Sally C. Curtin, 2016)

nearly 42,000 people successfully end their lives each year, and males take their own lives nearly four times the rate of females, representing 77.9% of all suicides. The most common suicide mechanism of choice for men is firearms. While I am angry with that husband and father who has taken his life, mainly because it seems to me to be such a selfish and thoughtless act, I have not considered an important point made by the CDC. Over 90 percent of people who die by suicide have a mental illness at the time of their death. And the most common mental illness is depression. Untreated depression is the number one cause for suicide. Over the years, my thoughts about this man have changed from anger to empathy. Now, I encourage men and concerned family members to seek out mental health assistance for the struggling men in their lives.

In 1999, I am a firefighter at Truck Company 9, but I am also assigned to the Med Unit (ambulance) #14 housed in that fire station. As a member of Med Unit 14, I am required to respond to all medical incidents dispatched to Med 14. One Saturday early afternoon, I am lounging nicely on the couch in the big TV room, shoes off and feet up, watching some college football. The knockout buzzer goes off for Med 14, dispatching us on a report of a 34-year-old female shot in the chest with unknown level of consciousness. I bounce up, landing in my shoes, and sprint to the ambulance. Paramedic Whiting jumps in the driver's seat and me in the front passenger's seat. I'm imagining all the blood that I am going to see splattered on the walls and floors, and I'm reflecting on my EMT training for the possible treatment of a gunshot wound to the chest. We arrive on the scene; a police officer is standing on the porch in the doorway, waving us to come in. We grab the bags; I'm expecting the worst.

We enter the apartment and walk to the rear into the back bedroom. We find the patient, a woman, sitting up in her bed, with her shirt raised above her bare breast. She is screaming at the top of her lungs because of the pain that she is experiencing. The police officer is just standing at ease--he's not looking for a suspected shooter; he's actually got a bit of a smirk on his face. Then I notice that there isn't a great amount of blood pouring out of the lady's body, she clearly hasn't been shot in the chest, and there is a gun positioned at the foot of this queen-sized bed.

Finally, Paramedic Whiting inquires, "What the hell happened!"

The lady stops her screaming long enough to explain with tears flowing, "I tried to kill myself."

Frustrated, Whiting asks, "How did you try to kill yourself?"

She continues, "I took the gun and placed it to my side, and pulled the trigger." I glance over at the side of her body, and sure enough, she's telling the truth. She shot herself in the side and there is an entrance hole and an exit hole in her body. I've never seen anything like it before. Though she is in excruciating pain, she is in virtually no danger of dying.

Paramedic Whiting rolls his eyes. "You mean to tell me that you wanted to kill yourself, so you got a gun and pointed it at your side?" He picks up the gun and literally places it under his chin. "Girl, if you want to kill yourself, don't shoot yourself in the side; you have to put that thing right up under your head and pull the trigger! That gets it done every time!"

"Whiting!" I shout with my eyes bugged out. The police officer visibly chuckles, and Whiting displays this mischievous grin, and immediately proceeds to caring for the distressed and embarrassed woman.

> **{Remember} "In general, firefighters have a warped, sometimes twisted, often times inappropriate and non-politically correct sense of humor. We beg your forgiveness."**

I know that the real reason Whiting is playing and being silly is in part to disguise his own anxiety, nervousness, frustration, and maybe even the darker side of his own struggles with depression. I know Whiting is facing real hurtful struggles in his marriage that are causing him to act out and be negative and cantankerous at work. Couple that with the pressure and anxiety of getting dispatched to a person that has supposedly been shot in the chest with all the possible complications that come with that type of trauma, and you have been tasked with the responsibility of saving that person's life. It can cause a person to do and say what they ought not, and to become less than the professional that they should be. Often, we see a friend, a coworker, a family member, or a neighbor stressed and overwhelmed, becoming cynical and negative, spiraling downward. And because of our personal fear of getting involved or not wanting to intrude, we do nothing. Then we are shocked to hear of the demise of their marriage, the loss of their job, or God forbid, even the news that they have taken their own or someone else's life.

> **{LESSON 10} "Be bold, get involved, exhibit the brave heart of a firefighter. Your involvement may actually save someone's life."**

There are three simple ways to intervene:

1. Offer the ministry of your presence – Be a good listening ear.

2. Be positive – When people are dwelling in a negative place, they need to be reminded of the good in life.

3. Offer your touch – When appropriate, there is nothing more comforting than a loving hug, an arm around their shoulder, a gentle squeeze of their hand, a light rub or pat on their back.

Paramedic Whiting made the huge mistake of underestimating and undervaluing this woman's resolve and level of commitment to her ending her own life. He made the classic mistake of considering her actions as just a way to get attention. He had not considered that she wasn't just making idle threats; she actually shot herself with a shotgun!

There are nearly 500,000 people with self-inflicted injuries treated in US emergency departments each year. In order to save our coworkers' and loved ones' lives. we must take their cries for help seriously and at face value, before they move from words to deadly action. I offer these simple preventative actions:

1. Learn the suicide warning signs, such as the person talking about wanting to hurt themselves, increasing substance use, changes in their mood, diet, or sleeping patterns.

2. When these warning signs appear, quickly connect the person to supportive services.

3. Promote opportunities and settings that strengthen the person's connections with caring people, families, and communities.

I had never met this lady before, nor did I have any background information concerning her family life or psychiatric history. I do know that despite her possible feelings of loneliness or despair, someone in the world loved that lady and would have been completely devastated at hearing of her demise. Therefore, I have always been extremely glad that she was unsuccessful in her attempted suicide.

I remember seeing the remnants of a person who attempted suicide with a shotgun and didn't survive to talk about it. It was around 2009; I am working as the company commander (in charge of a firefighter crew) at Engine 5, one of our busy downtown fire companies. The city streets are bustling with lots of traffic, especially due to a massive gun show convention in town. Engine 5 is dispatched to one of the high-end hotel properties in downtown Louisville, on a report of a man shot. There are no further details or information given, except that Louisville Metro Police are also responding.

We arrive to this beautiful hotel setting, and this gorgeous hotel lobby where so many individuals are mingling with cocktail drinks in hand, and just having an overall good time. Unbeknownst to all of these seemingly blissful conference attendees, just a few floors above their heads, one of their own members has for some reason decided that he can no longer endure life, and has purposefully ended his life with the very tool that they are all at the conference to commemorate. As we arrive to what I remember being the sixth floor, we can see the police standing in the doorway of the victim's hotel room. As we come to the door, one of the officers give me the universal facial sign that we are about to see something grotesque. The officer's lips smash together, and his nose crinkles, and he wags his head slowly and says, "There ain't nothing you guys can do for this one."

I tell my guys to wait in the hallway, and I walk in. My eyes are immediately drawn to the second queen bed in the room, the one nearest to the window, and see the remains of a man supine (lying flat on his back) with most of his face and head missing, and what looks like vomit on the walls, but is actually the splattering of this man's brains and bodily fluids and tissue. It is easy to ascertain that this man had sat at the foot of his bed, and with the pull of a trigger, ended his life. What looks like a pump-action shotgun sits near the side of the bed in plain view. I am so mesmerized by the contrasting beauty of this hotel room and the gruesomeness of the scene, that I am a bit startled by the voices that emanate from the bathroom. It is another police officer, and she is interviewing the victim's roommate. The man's face was as white and pale as the man's skin lying on the bed. He is visibly shaken and disturbed by the obvious suicide of his friend. But his recounting of the previous moments grip me.

He explains in slow-motion detail, "We had just come back up to the room. We had been laughing and talking the whole way. Jeff [not his real name] went and sat on his bed and had started taking his shoes off. I walked into the bathroom and shut the door. There was silence for a few minutes and, and," the man pauses midsentence, "...the gun goes off." He continues, "I opened the door, and there he was ... I just hollered at him, Jeff why did you do that," the man holds his arms out at the dead man lying on the bed, as if he has life and consciousness to hear, "Jeff, why did you do this, man!"

At this point, I realize that the first officer that spoke to me at the door was right; there isn't anything I can do for either of these men. So, I quickly exit the room. But the somber, painful question of the man in the bathroom to his friend lying dead on the bed haunts my thoughts to this day: "WHY?" What could have been so terrible that a man who obviously had some positives in his life, at least one friend who loved him, and felt close enough to travel together, share a room together, experience some memories and laughs together, would end his life in the very near presence of his friend. WHY? This incident has caused me to observe and consider the behavior and the mental and emotional state of my wife, my children, my family and friends, and my coworkers in a way that I had never previously contemplated or examined. More than anything, I never want to be like the man in the bathroom whose door was shut to the true mental state of his friend, and whose eyes weren't open to see the truth until it was too late.

As I relate these stories, I hope that no one thinks that I am building a case against guns. I am neither a gun-holder nor a gun-hater; I suspect that a gun in and of itself is not good or evil, but just like any other tool or mechanism, its purpose is established and determined by the hands that hold it.

> **{LESSON 11} "I am neither a gun-holder nor a gun-hater, I suspect that a gun in and of itself is not good or evil, but just like any other tool or mechanism; its purpose is established and determined by the hands that hold it."**

I am simply sharing some scenarios that firefighters and first responders experience on a daily basis. Unfortunately, gun violence is an everyday situational reality for many communities and many firefighters that serve them. Most of the time, firefighters are called to respond to incidents and treat victims who have been injured by gunfire, but increasingly, first responders are becoming the target of terrorist-minded or mentally deranged individuals. One fall evening in 1996, my second year on the fire department, I am detailed to Engine 12 in the south end of Louisville. It has been a fairly slow work day, with no major incidents to speak of. Around seven o'clock in the evening, we have just finished eating dinner and are washing the dishes and cleaning the kitchen, when we are dispatched on a medical incident on a report of a forty-year-old female with general sickness. Let me just be honest, firefighters respond to a number of medical incidents that cause our adrenaline to go into hyper drive; "general sickness" is not one of those. Not to mention, the captain that is in-charge of Engine 12 is a man that at the time, looking at him with my 21-year-old eyes, I thought he was nearly eighty years old (he was actually in his late forties). Needless to say, we are in no great hurry.

When we arrive, Captain Nard and another firefighter make their way up the porch steps to the front door of this one-story shotgun house, while I grab the red medical bag and the orange-cased oxygen bottle from the outside fire truck compartment. There is a small porch light that illuminates an unkempt elderly man sitting in the right-hand corner of the porch, sipping from a beer can. The glare of the yellow porch light, and the cigarette smoke rising from his ashtray, make the old man sitting in that wooden rocking chair look even creepier.

As Captain Nard enters the house, I can hear the old man mumbling something, but I am not close enough yet to actually make out what he is saying. I guess Captain Leonard doesn't understand the man either, because they just walk straight inside the house. When I reach the porch, I greet the old man. "Good evening, sir."

The old man mumbles to me with a raspy voice, barely looking up at me, "I told them boys she's crazy and she got a gun."

I pause in the doorway, and looking back at him, I ask, "What did you say, sir?"

He speaks up, rough but clearer, "My daughter is crazy as hell, and she got a gun!"

He hardly finishes his sentence, when Captain Nard and the other firefighter come bolting out of the house. "She's got a gun and she's counting to three!"

I really could hardly catch what they were saying, and I never saw the gun, but when I saw old Captain Nard moving faster than I have ever imagined he could, I knew that the warning the creepy old man on the porch gave us must have been true; that lady must have a gun! Without hesitation, and with the medical bag and oxygen tank in hand, I jump the five porch steps and high-step back to the fire truck. I don't bother to place the equipment back into the compartments; we just hop into the cab (interior seating area) and slam the doors shut.

Captain Nard screams at the confused sergeant who is sitting in the driver's seat, "Go, go, go!" And with that, we speed off faster and with more enthusiasm than we arrived with; I guess that lady didn't want our help. To this day, that was the most thrilling, adrenaline-filled "general sickness" incident that I have ever been dispatched to. After that night, I had a greater appreciation and respect for the danger of every incident that we handle and for the swift speed of old Captain Nard.

CHAPTER 9
Animal Planet

When most people think of firefighters and animals, they normally consider three animals; horses, dogs, and cats. [10]The time from the Civil War to the early 1920s could be known in firefighting as the era of the fire horse. Prior to that time, firefighters were required to pull the fire wagons that transported the water tanks, ladders and equipment. When fire horses were introduced, they were lauded by firefighters as noble, powerful team members, and they were much beloved by the public. They were often very well treated and exceptionally groomed.

[11]The second animal consider must be the Dalmatian Dog, perhaps best known for working for firefighters in the role as firefighting apparatus escorts and firehouse mascots. Since Dalmatians and horses are very compatible, the dogs were easily trained to run in front of the fire department horse-drawn carriages to help clear a path and quickly guide the horses and firefighters to the fires. Dalmatians are often

---

10   (Longaberger, 2012)
11   (Paramedic)

considered to make good watchdogs, and they may have been useful to fire brigades as guard dogs to protect a firehouse and its equipment. Fire engines used to be drawn by fast and powerful horses, a tempting target for thieves, so Dalmatians were kept in the firehouse as deterrence to theft. Finally, I mention cats only because of all of the supposed "cat in a tree" rescues.

Over my twenty-three years of fire service, I have never worked with a horse, nor possessed a Dalmatian dog or any other dog at any of my fire stations. Furthermore, I have never rescued a cat from a tree. But in this animal planet that we live in, every firefighter will surely walk into situations and encounter animal species that could not have been anticipated when they showed up for their 24-hour shift.

Have I ever rescued a cat from a tree? No. But on a cold, stormy autumn night Engine 10 was dispatched to an apartment complex, where someone reported hearing a baby crying on top of the roof. When we arrive, there are about five adults standing in the rain, congregating next to the building, looking and pointing up toward the roof of the building. As we all exit the fire truck, we are all thinking the same thing you are thinking now: "How and why would a baby be on top of the roof of an apartment building?"

The captain yells out to me and the other firefighter to grab the thirty-foot ladder. Once we have the ladder, we carry it toward the building and extend it about four rungs past the roof line. Once it is raised and positioned, the captain immediately climbs to the roof, with me following right behind him. As soon as we step onto the roof, we can see a black plastic garbage bag, tied at the top, with something moving around in it. We can hear what sound like the whimpers of a baby.

The captain grabs the bag, and rips it open and pulls out a wet, frightened gray kitten. Some cruel, heartless, despicable person stuffed that kitten alive in a trash bag to die a slow, stressful death. But once again, the good in others prevailed over evil. These neighbors didn't sit around waiting for someone else to handle it, but they took action; they took the time to help, to intervene.

Speaking of the good and helpfulness of others, in 2003 I was a firefighter assigned to Truck company 4. It was a bright, sunny afternoon in Beautiful West Louisville, when Truck 4 was dispatched to a medical incident with a report of a man mauled by a dog. Approximately fifteen minutes prior to our dispatch, two men in their mid-late forties were walking eastward down an alley heading to a friend's house. As they had walked nearly halfway down the alley, two massive 120-pound pit bull dogs had just escaped from their inadequate enclosure and entered the alley from someone's back yard. The two men spotted the dogs before the dogs had a chance to take notice of them, so they quietly turned back to try and exit the alley from the direction that they had entered. At some point, the two ferocious-looking pit bulls looked up and saw the two men, and immediately broke into a full sprint toward the retreating men. The two men immediately dropped the bags that they were carrying, and utilized every old, outdated muscles that they possessed in their bodies to help perpetuate their escape. They were running down an alley that was the rear parking lot area to an abandoned elementary school. The school had just been purchased by a developer that had plans to renovate the dilapidated structure and had erected a massive ten-foot chain-link fence to prevent vagrants from trespassing.

When the men realized that they were not going to be able

to outrun the fast-approaching dogs, they decide, to climb over the ten-foot-high construction fence. Both men stumbled over the top of the fence and reached the other side just as as the dogs arrived. As they stood on the grass-filled concrete parking lot, out of breath yet feeling somewhat secure, the two pit bulls arrived at the men's position at the fence, and without hesitation leapt onto the fence and began to scale it. Now, the two men started to quickly scurry to the opposite side of the parking lot, nearly 200 feet away, where they would then have to climb the ten-foot fence for the second time. The two men were screaming for anyone to help. The first man arrived at the fence, and within seconds ascended up and over to safety. The second man made it across the parking lot with pit bulls growling and barking behind him as he reached the fence successfully. But he was totally worn out, and his ascent up the fence was slow and strenuous. He reached his arm toward the top of the fence when the first pit bull leaped toward the fence and attached his colossal teeth and jaws around the man's right leg, tearing straight through his calf, halting his upward progress. A moment later, the second pit vaulted up with a single leap and fastened his fangs into the man's upper thigh and buttocks, forcing the man off the fence. The dogs began to inflict tremendous injury to the man, biting and tearing flesh from his body mercilessly.

As he writhed in bloody pain on the concrete, he screamed out for help, for someone to rescue him. "Help, help! Somebody help me!! They're killing me! They're killing me!"

The man's friend stood on the other side of the fence, paralyzed with fear, without the will to reenter the lion's den, also screaming for help, for a rescuer. While the dogs continued their vicious attack, a thin, but athletic-built man, a [12]"Good Samaritan," a [13]"Kingsman" armed with just an umbrella, surged up and over the fence and began his courageous defense of the fallen victim. He swatted, smacked, kicked, and roared against the pit bulls, until they ended their assault and retreated away from the crime scene.

Upon Truck 4's arrival, we find the victim with thirty-seven bite wounds to his face, head, arms, legs, buttocks, chest, back, and places where whole chunks of flesh were taken from his body, but thank God, he was still alive. We start to bandage and treat his wounds. In a shaky, nervous, excitable voice, the patient begins to describe to us the nightmare, "They tried to kill me! They tried to kill me! The big one tried to put his mouth around my throat!" Overcome with emotion, he begins to weep, "They almost killed me, if it wasn't for this man!" With big teardrops streaming down his face, he points to his rescuer, "This man saved my life. You saved me, man. Thank you, man, thank you."

That's when it hits me, the beauty of what this man did. The victim had no name for his rescuer, because the rescuer was a true Good Samaritan, a stranger that answers a cry for help, disregarding his own well-being. In the biblical story found in Matthew Chapter Ten, the Good Samaritan sees a man attacked and severely beaten by a gang of robbers; the man is left to die in the street. Many people pass by the man, unwilling to get involved. But the Good Samaritan sees this person to whom he has no relationship or obligation--just a fellow human being in need, and shows compassion. He takes time out of a busy schedule, reaches down, gets the hands dirty,

12   (Matthew)
13   (Matthew Vaughn, 2014)

and spends his own capital to rescue someone in distress. This is the true spirit and calling of those in the fire profession – selfless, courageous, compassionate service to our fellow man in distress. I never did catch this rescuer's name, but today, on this page, I present to him "THE FIREFIGHTER SPIRIT AWARD" for selfless, courageous, compassionate service! And I challenge each of you reading these pages to become more selfless, more courageously compassionate toward your neighbor, coworker, classmate, or a stranger in need.

{LESSON 12} "The true spirit of a firefighter is a Good Samaritan, a stranger that answers a cry for help, disregarding one's own wellbeing."

This wouldn't be my last encounter with large, vicious dogs. I was working in the south end of Louisville at Station 12. Around 9:00 in the morning, in the early spring of 2006, I am the captain assigned as the in-charge member of Engine 12 when the company is dispatched on an incident with a report of a police officer injured by an animal. Approximately, fifteen minutes before our dispatch, the police officer stepped out of bed, still in his pajamas, and took his two little white poodle dogs through his tiny apartment-sized kitchen, to the back door that led to the back yard, so that the dogs could relieve themselves. He left the door open so that the poodles could come back into the house when they were ready. The officer walked back through the house to the front door to retrieve the morning newspaper. He then returned to the kitchen, walked over to the cabinets and the refrigerator, and got his cereal and milk. He came over to the two-person kitchen table and sat down. With his right hand, he scooped up delicious bites of cereal and milk, and with his left hand he held the morning newspaper to his face. He then heard the poodles in the back yard barking and squealing, but he ignored them, because he thought the dogs must be chasing or killing a squirrel.

While he continued to enjoy his breakfast and paper, the female poodle darted back through the kitchen, yelping at the top of her voice. As he caught just a glimpse of her speeding body turning the corner out of the kitchen, he thought he noticed blood on her white hair. Before he could react to this, a 130-pound, black and brown Rottweiler dog burst through the back door and brushed past his leg in full pursuit of the female poodle. Apparently, when the Rottweiler heard the two dogs enter the back yard, he dug beneath the wooden privacy fence, went into full attack mode, and chased the two poodles into the back corner of the yard. He then killed the male poodle and was coming after the female to finish the job. The officer, without hesitation, sprang into action to save his remaining pet. He just so happened to keep his service gun in the kitchen. Just as he got the gun loaded, the poodle returned to the kitchen and straight between officer's protective legs. The Rottweiler also returned, snarling toward the dog and the officer. He shot the dog once in the side, and the dog kept advancing, so he placed two more strategic shots into the Rot, and he finally lay over on his side, dead.

When the Engine 12 crew and I arrive, we are surprised by the scene of a dead Rottweiler on this man's kitchen floor (it's a sight that you don't see every day.) We have been dispatched for an injured officer, so I ask the man whether the dog injured him? He shows me his bleeding hand, but explains that the dog didn't bite or have a chance to even touch him, but that he scraped his hand on the box that was holding his gun. While he holds his pet poodle in his arms, I can sense his sorrow for the loss of his male pet, but he is obviously grateful that he was able to rescue the remaining dog.

I don't know if you are keeping track, but the score is Vicious Dogs 1 – Humans 1, and I'm about to give you the tie-breaker.

It is the first cold night of the late fall season in Louisville, which is normally the first night that most people feel the need to turn on their furnaces, and this is before most ever get their furnace serviced. Most experienced firefighters know that's a recipe for a house fire. That night, I am working as a firefighter on Truck 7 when we are dispatched on a full box alarm (three engine companies, two truck companies, and one battalion chief) – house fire. Truck 7 is the second truck company on the scene, so our responsibility upon arrival to the scene of the burning residential house is to pull through the back alley and attack the fire from the rear.

My captain yells back at me from the front seat, "Ford, grab the room ladder!"

"Yes, sir," I respond.

The room ladder is a six-foot A-frame metal ladder that has the capability to be extended into a straight-beam ladder that is perfectly fitted to access attic spaces; it's a fire ground necessity. So as we come to a stop, I can see that most of the fire is in the the front first floor of this two-story wood-frame home. I exit the truck with my ax and my plaster hook in my left hand and immediately go to the rear of the apparatus and open the room ladder compartment, and pull the room ladder from off the truck. I am of course wearing my SCBA (Self-Contained Breathing Apparatus) that has shoulder straps and a waist strap. I slide the handle of my ax in between the SCBA waist straps to free up my left hand so I just have to carry the six-foot plaster hook (some call it a pike pole – a long metal-topped wood, aluminum, or fiberglass pole used for reaching, pulling and tearing through ceilings, roofs, etc.) and I can place the six-foot, fifty-pound room ladder on my right shoulder as I hurry to keep up with my captain, who is already heading toward the burning house.

The captain and I gather ourselves and kneel down at the back door of the house to don our SCBA face pieces. We make entry into the residence standing up; there isn't a need to crawl on our knees, because the heat is minimal. Visibility is less than zero; the noise level is excessive, as usual in a house fire, due to sirens, alarms, the crashing into furniture, the breaking of windows, and of course the shouting firefighters (we may not be able to see each other, but we can touch and shout in order not to lose one another in the blackness). You can't see your hand in front of your face from the intense black smoke.

We make our way into what I believe is the front first-floor dining room. My captain shouts, "Michael, I think we have some fire in the ceiling!"

"Yes, sir!" I reply.

I know he's actually telling me to use my plaster hook to open the ceiling and search for fire extension. So I do. I start pulling the ceiling down. My captain shouts at me again. "Michael, I going to check the room across the hall!"

"Yes, sir!" I reply as I continue pulling.

I realize that the engine crews must have knocked down (extinguished) the main body of fire, and the truck personnel must have completed adequate ventilation, because the visibility is becoming clearer. As I'm pulling the ceiling, I have this feeling that I'm not the only one in the room. I glance to my right and I'm startled by what looks like a full grown, three-foot-tall Rottweiler dog sitting up against the wall about ten feet from my position! I stop pulling ceilings, take a good look, and ready myself for an attack, but the thing never moves; it just stands there staring. I laugh at myself for being frightened--it's just one of those dumb dog statues. I continue with my assignment. Moments later, I glance over at the Rottweiler dog statue again, and it is still sitting, but no longer against the wall; it's now about five feet closer. Jesus! That's a real Rottweiler dog, and he's sneaking up on me for the attack.

I drop my pike pole and reach for the fire ax that's on my waist. Now the dog and I just stare at each other for a few seconds. I then realize he's not on the attack; he's just disoriented by the smoke and confused by the the alien being, dressed in glowing fire gear from head to toe, pulling down ceilings. So the ferocious dog and the human make a truce, I go over to him, grab him by the collar and lead him outdoors. The paramedics even place an oxygen mask on him to help clear his head. For a moment, that Rottweiler dog actually looked cute and grateful. Well, on this day, we found out that perhaps Man and Beast can coexist with each other in the spirit of harmony.

Speaking of harmony between Man and Beast, I never knew how warm and intimate the two could become, until one winter morning as I arrived for my shift around seven o'clock. I had been promoted to sergeant and was now assigned to Engine Company 7, the oldest operating fire station in the country at the time. The station had opened in 1871, and in 2007 the structure had seen better days. Nonetheless, I loved the place; it was home for me and thirteen other firefighters every third day. The old gravel parking lot was in the rear of the station, and I would make my morning entrance through the back door that led directly into the kitchen. The kitchen was always the hub of activity, because it served as the cooking and eating area, complete with a refrigerator and Vulcan stove and an eight-person table; it was also the company library, complete with a bookshelf full of firefighting, hazmat, medical, and water-pumping books; it was also the television room with a huge flat-screen TV purchased by the firefighters' pooled money.

And for some firefighters it also served as their bedroom. Sure, there was a humongous 25-person bedroom on the second floor where most of the fire company members rested. But some firefighters never get comfortable sleeping in what we refer to in each fire station as the "Big Room." It's understandable; sleeping in the "Big Room" is not your normal situation. I mean, most home bedrooms are not the size of a small church sanctuary, with the cathedral glass windows to match. Most home bedrooms don't have four to ten men and women farting, sneezing, coughing, snoring, horse playing, or performing practical jokes throughout the night. Ultimately, some firefighters never get used to the fire alarm waking them out of a dead sleep, sometimes every hour of the night, and having to slide the twenty-foot pole, or run down the thirty-five steps in order to make it to the apparatus, get dressed, and be out the door in one minute and thirty seconds. So for these firefighters, the downstairs couch is the best solution--that's why we call them "Couchers."

I'm not surprised that morning as I arrive to find firefighter Mick, a definite Coucher. asleep on the kitchen couch. Mick is a tall, very fit man, a little strange at times, but an overall nice guy. I'm not going to pay the sleeping firefighter to much attention, as I have come in a little early to make myself a little breakfast. But I can't help noticing how silly Mick looks, asleep and snuggling with a fuzzy gray stuffed toy animal. It's almost time for him to wake up anyway, so I call his name, "Mick, hey Mick." I do this calmly so I don't startle him.

"Hey Sarge, what's up?" he answers me groggily and without moving anything but his eyes.

I chuckle, "You look awfully cute with that stuffed bear under your arm."

He looks confused. "What stuffed bear?"

"Under your armpit," I explain.

Without actually looking, he reaches his right hand over to his left armpit and pulls the stuffed bear out from under his arms, except it wiggles and squeals softly as he holds it up with his bare hands. His eyes pop out, and my eyes and mouth drop to the floor! It's a real baby possum! Firefighter Mick throws the creature in the air and screams like a sixteen-year-old girl, and I join him. The cute baby possum somehow strolled inside from the cold and searched for the warmest, best place to spend the night. He made his decision that the "Big Room" wasn't his speed; the baby possum was a Coucher. And I thank God, because the "Big Room" would not be big enough for me and that creature. I could handle farting, sneezing, coughing, snoring, horse playing, and practical jokes, but not a baby possum--I would need to be reassigned to a different station! Fortunately for me and the baby possum, we find his mother sleeping under a shed near the alley.

Now, don't get me wrong, I actually love animals. In fact, one of my most exciting and enjoyable days on the Louisville Fire Department came in May of 2010. I had been promoted to captain, and was in-charge of Quint Company 9, located in the Poplar Level Road area of South Louisville, near German Town. I have just arrived from working late at another station the night before. It is around eight o'clock in the morning; I review the captain's log book, and the entry from the captain that I'm relieving states that my crew and shift are scheduled for a 10:00 a.m. walk through of the Louisville Zoo's newly renovated animal exhibition areas. I am pretty pumped to see the zoo on the schedule--Louisville has one of the most outstanding zoos in the country. It's a place that I've taken my five children at least a hundred times, but since now they are all teenagers, we haven't visited the zoo in years. So, I conduct morning roll call with my sergeant and two firefighters, reviewing the company log book and staff memos, giving out assignments, and inform them that we are to conduct a ten o'clock walkthrough at the zoo. Morning roll call is usually very informal, laid-back, and conversational.

Firefighter Yack says, "Oh yeah, Cap, how was your East Africa trip?"

My face lights up and I begin to give the details of my trip. "Aw man, it was wonderful!" I explain how my wife and I and our five children visited some Kenyan elementary schools that we support financially on a monthly basis, how all of us taught classes at the schools, and how well my children learned the Swahili language. I tell them that one of the best parts of the entire trip was the three days of safari on the 583-square-mile Masai Mara National Game Reserve. The mountainous landscape views were inspiring, the lions, giraffes, hyenas, buffalo, wildebeests, jaguars, cheetahs, rhinos, hippopotamus, zebras, and gazelles were each equally impressive. But to see the massive, regal elephants in herds of fifties, and strolling through the fields in slow motion, was flat-out breathtaking. The elephants were hands down our favorite creature.

Firefighter Yack chimes in, "Cap, I have a friend who's one of the elephant trainers at the zoo, and if you want to, when we walk through the zoo today, I will check and see if he will let you go into the elephant enclosure to see the elephants up close."

"Really?" I react, with my face beaming like a little kid's. Now I'm truly excited. So, I end the roll call meeting, the sergeant finishes the morning apparatus checks, the firefighters accomplish their morning firehouse cleaning chores, and I complete payroll and the employee attendance/scheduling. By 9:45 we are all clean-shaven, shoes polished, in our uniform of the day, and boarding the Quint 9 apparatus. The Louisville Zoo is about three minutes north of the fire station, so we arrive fairly quickly. The zoo manager meets us at the gate to allow us into the rear maintenance area. We make entry through the rear access door, where there is a full-grown male lion, lying in what looks to me like a thin chain-link fence. The zookeepers say the lion is sick and that the fence can hold him adequately, but I move forward quickly inside the building, just in case they could be wrong about the strength of this cage.

But as I enter the building, I am immediately awe struck by two beautiful golden, black-spotted female cheetahs that are in smaller chain-link fences that look more like dog kennels. These two gorgeous female cats lie regally with their bodies stretched out and their heads postured upward; I step nearer for a closer look. Before I can make a complete step near the cage, these two deceivers rush toward me with lightning speed, hissing like two wicked witches. I almost fall backwards, attempting to change directions away from the cage. My guys get a good giggle out of my sudden fright.

We continue our tour, past the tiger enclosure, the polar bear house with its two full-grown polar bears and newborn cub, the zebras, the giraffes, and finally to the gorilla experience, where we are able to see twelve rainforest gorillas, including two silverbacks. The keeper tells us to remove our hats and bow our heads as we walk through the rear of the gorilla enclosure so that the massive silver gorilla won't feel threatened. I'm thinking, *He's five foot five tall, nearly 600 pounds of teeth and muscles, and she's worried about him feeling threatened?* I remove my cap, and bow my head as low as I could. I stop at the section where the cage turns to thick glass, and watch two smaller gorillas sitting together. *They are so cute*, I think, until one squeezes a long nasty chunk out of his butt, and the other one picks it up with his bare hands, looks over at me, and takes a big hefty bite, like it is a nutritious morning snack. When he sees the utter disgust on my face, he smiles and stuffs the remaining poo poo sandwich into his mouth.

Of course, while on the tour we review evacuation plans, fire suppression systems, fire alarm systems, and the overall hazardous materials content. When the tour is finished, Firefighter Yak introduces me to his friend, the elephant keeper. We enter the elephant house, and the keeper explains the simple ground rules: follow his lead, let the elephants come to you, and stay clear of the baby elephant because he's the most dangerous. The keeper tells us that the baby elephant is extremely playful and doesn't yet understand its own strength and weight. The keeper asks who all wants to go in. Firefighter Yack has been in before and the other two guys are too nervous, so they decline. But I look like a little kid, with my hand in the air, who knows the right answer to the teacher's question: "Me, me, me!" I have been seeing these two African elephants since I was a child and have taken my children many times to see these two Louisville Zoo celebrities, Mikki and Punch-- and the baby elephant, Scotty, is a Louisville mega-star.

As I enter, my heart is pounding out of my chest. You know these animals are mammoth, but you can't grasp their true size until you are standing next to them. Mikki, the female elephant, walks directly to me and lays her long trunk onto my right shoulder as I face her. She purrs gently and caresses my face. The two keepers smile and say, "She likes you." I know that elephants have incredible memories, so I like to think she just remembered me from all those visits when I came and sat on the bench outside of the enclosure and we just watched each other. Maybe she is just happy to finally meet me in person. Well, then Scotty, the baby elephant, gets past the keeper and runs toward me, and gives me a light brush to let me know that's his momma, and he wants some attention too. We snap a few pictures, and finally make our exit. As, I'm leaving, I think, *How great it is to be a firefighter! When I started the day, I never could have imagined the day would have involved these close encounters with the most famous animals on the planet, but such is the 24 hours of a firefighter, and the day is still young; we have sixteen hours left in this 24.*

Nearly a week later, I am driving in to work listening to the morning news on the radio and the reporter announces the saddest news. "The Louisville Zoo is saddened to report the death of Scotty the baby elephant." They explain that they are still running tests to determine the cause of Scotty's death. Wow! I think about those wonderful zookeepers, and Mikki the momma elephant. They must be devastated.

When I arrive to the fire station, Firefighter Yack meets me at the side door nearest to the parking lot. He has a very serious and distraught look on his face. "Hey Cap, we need to talk."

We step into my office, and Yack shuts the door behind us. He starts, "I just got a call from my zookeeper friend; he tells me that Scotty the elephant died last night."

I interrupt, "Yeah, I heard on the radio this morning--they said that the zoo doesn't know what he died of."

Yack jumps in, "That's just it, they do know how he died!" he says with an intense look of mystery.

"How?" I ask.

He continues, "My friend, the zookeeper, said that somehow there were traces of African dirt that got mixed with the dirt in the elephant enclosure. That African dirt had some kind of diseased microorganisms that got into Scotty's body and killed him." Then with judgmentally intense eyes he asks me, "Didn't you tell me that you just got back from traveling around in Africa?"

The guiltiest feeling that I have ever felt overtakes my mind. "Yes, I did just get back from Africa, but that was weeks before we visited the elephants," my guilty conscious tries to explain. But I'm wondering--did I kill Baby Scotty?! When I heard the news on the radio this morning on my way into work for my 24-hour shift, I never could have imagined that the death/murder investigation of Louisville's first baby elephant in fifty years could lead back to me! While I am struggling with guilty worry on my face, Firefighter Yack can no longer contain himself; he bursts out with laughter. "I'm just kidding! He didn't die from African dirt!" I want to punch him right in the throat, but that was a good one. He definitely got me! I mean really, "African dirt!" I'm not normally this gullible, but the initial horror that I may have been the cause of a baby elephant dying caused my mind to go into a brief analysis paralysis.

I eventually shake myself from the brain freeze and realize that during our zoo tour, I was wearing my fire department black work boots that had never touched African soil. "I'm a stinking idiot, you got me!"

See, this is what I have been trying to enlighten you on concerning firefighters. Only a firefighter would take comedic license and capitalize on a such a sensitive topic as the death of a baby elephant on the day it's announced.

{REMEMBER} "In general, firefighters have a warped, sometimes twisted, often times inappropriate and non-politically correct sense of humor. We beg your forgiveness."

CHAPTER 10
Domestic Encounters

Some of the most difficult incidents that confront firefighters each day are domestic incidents. On these occasions, when we arrive to a home sometimes we find family clashes, skirmishes, fights, abuse, and even murder. These events are some of the most emotionally charged atmospheres that make the firefighters' job difficult, challenging, and sometimes more dangerous than an actual house fire.

Early one Thursday evening, I am the in-charge member of Engine Company 5 when we respond to a domestic 911 call at an apartment complex in downtown Louisville. The dispatch simply says that the wife of a fifty-six-year-old man called and reported that her husband had multiple injuries, but would not say what the injuries were nor how the injuries occurred. When Engine 5 arrives, the Med Unit pulls up to the scene just as we're exiting the fire truck. We assist the med crew with carrying the medical bags and pushing the stretcher bed to the apartment. There is a police officer on the scene, and she lets us know that the scene is secure and it's okay to enter. Upon entry, we find the fifty-six-year-old man lying quietly on the bedroom floor. He has obviously been viciously attacked by someone. His head and face are severely bruised with large contusions. His body has nearly twenty large hematomas from his upper torso down to his tibia (shin bone), including what appear to be a broken rib and a broken hip. As the man lies surprisingly quiet, I ask him what happened to him.

He immediately begins to offer a series of excuses. "She didn't mean it, I provoked her, this was my fault. I love you, baby!" the man shouts toward the woman sitting in a chair in the hallway directly outside of the bedroom.

We all turn our eyes on the woman as she sits with a very stoic yet slightly distraught look on her face. The police officer chimes in with the details. "Apparently Mr. Foster was upset with his wife concerning something to do with dinner not being prepared to his liking and decided to strike his wife in the face. Apparently, his striking his wife is a frequent occurrence. Mrs. Foster waited until Mr. Foster her husband lay in the bed and fell asleep, and she took that Louisville Slugger baseball bat--" the officer pointed to the bat standing in the corner of the room "--and beat him with it."

As the officer explains, the wife begins to sob softly. And the injured man starts up again, "Don't cry, baby; this is all my fault. I shouldn't have hit you again, I won't do it anymore. Officer, I don't want to press charges."

We quickly bandage and immobilize the man, preparing him for transport, understanding that this man is truly in critical condition, with life-threatening injuries. After we load him onto the stretcher, we open the apartment door to exit, and we are met by an extremely high-spirited and angry mob of nearly fifty residents of the apartment complex.

They stand on the walkway that we need to travel to get the man to the ambulance, and they purposely impede our access. They begin screaming at the man, "Now, that's what you get, you mean bastard! It's about time she whipped your butt! She should have completely beat your head in! She should have finished the job!"

I'm completely shocked by this crowd and completely stunned by the depth of their vehement resentment of this man. In sixteen years on the fire department, I have never seen anything like this. The mob's hatred of this man turns against the firefighters and the EMS workers, because we are helping the man. The crowd shouts at us, "Don't help him! Let him die! He deserves to die!" I really need that police officer right about now, but I realize that she is still in the apartment with the man's wife. So I look the mob leaders in the eyes and explain to them in a gentle but firm voice, "We are firefight-ers. We are here to help--we wouldn't let you, him, or anyone just die without trying to help." And with that, they let us pass through to the ambulance.

We travel lights and sirens to University Hospital, one of the best trauma hospitals in the country, were he is taken to Room 9 (Emergency Intensive Care Unit). I would like to tell you that the man lived, but I don't know. I would love to tell you that the wife wasn't incarcerated, but I don't know. I would love to tell you that the husband never hit her again, but I don't know. I would love to tell you that this couple solved their problems and that they lived happily ever after, but I don't know, and frankly, I seriously doubt it. But truth is that one of the most difficult aspects of the firefighter's pro-fession is that much of the work we do comes without closure. We enter some of the most challenging times in people's lives, we connect with them through this forced intimacy, get them through to a certain point in a situation, then we turn them over to someone else--the police, a medical crew, the hospital, or the coroner. And just like that, the story for us ends, without any closure. I guess sometimes that's good, because many times we walk away feeling we made a difference and we never find out that ultimately our work was actually ineffective or futile. You know, out of all the drama of this incident there was one thing that I continued to ponder in my mind. When the wife started to cry, what was she crying about? Was she remorseful for nearly killing her husband? Was it relief for finally giving him a dose of his own medicine? Was it regret for putting up with his abuse for so many years? Or was she touched in some way because he finally took responsibility for how he had abused her? At any rate, this wouldn't be the last time that I would see two people who loved each other but who physically hurt each other.

{Forced Intimacy} "When firefighters enter into people's lives in emergency situations and find them in their most vulnerable states; sick, injured, naked, bleeding, covered in vomit or feces, etc."

It is a moonlit, late-spring evening and I am working the midnight shift on Med Unit 20. We respond to a domestic incident in the charming Highlands area of east Louisville. Dispatch reports that two males were fighting, and one was stabbed with a knife. When we arrive, we find that Metro Louisville Police has already secured the scene, and the apparent attacker is in handcuffs, sitting on the living room floor. The apartment is immaculately furnished and decorated, but there seems to be blood spilled and splattered everywhere. The two men have evidently been lovers for quite some time, but for some reason got into a verbal argument on this night, which concluded in one stabbing the other with a meat cleaver. When we reach the victim, he is sitting on the kitchen floor; he is fully conscious and alert, but he has a ten-inch butcher's knife still stuck in between his neck and his shoulder. There is a fat piece of shoulder muscle dangling and dripping with blood. The sight of it makes my stomach flutter and and a bit queasy. As we begin to briskly package the man for transport to the emergency room, both the men have had a moment to calm down from the heat of whatever the argument was about, so the man in handcuffs begins to certainly feel remorse for the injury that he has caused.

He says to the man on the stretcher, "This was stupid. We shouldn't fight over stupid stuff!"

The man on the stretcher nods his head in agreement. They both apologize to each other, and as we whisk the patient out to the ambulance and off to the hospital, the man in the handcuffs shouts "I love you!." The man in handcuffs, who stabbed his lover, surely felt a great sense of remorse for what he did to the person he claimed to love. Yet, how can you say with your mouth, "I love you," but with your actions, physically mutilate the man, as if you were worst enemies? This is a kind of love that I personally reject and refuse to define as love.

{LESSON 13} "Love suffers long and is kind... does not behave rudely...love is not provoked." (I Corinthians 13:4); "Love does no harm to a neighbor." (Romans 13:10)

Mot, shaking his head says, "You guys are going to hate me for this one."

I'm not quite sure what Mot means, but in my three short years on the department, I have never seen a paramedic come out to meet us with an apology before we even get started assisting. Mot then informs us as he leads us through the yard gate entrance, "The patient is in the back of the house."

As soon as we enter the yard, a foul, gross odor singes the hair in our noses. The odor smells like a toxic airborne pathogen of decaying maggot-filled roadkill and fresh dog poo that sticks in the cracks of your tennis shoes. It was nauseating, and we had not even ventured into the house. The entire way through the front yard, Paramedic Mot apologizes profusely, and so I'm guessing that this isn't the worst part. When Mot opens the front door, all of us nearly gag as the pathogen smacks us in the face. We are escorted by an older woman (maybe in her early sixties) through the living area of a very well-kept home. We arrive at the kitchen, where there is a half-naked woman lying on the floor. The woman is wearing a shirt, but she is not wearing any clothes or underclothes to cover her naked bottom. She is a very big lady, extremely overweight. She is actually lying in a two-inch-deep pool of her own intestinal waste. The rainbow of browns, yellows, and green sloppy muck covers the five-foot-square area where the woman is lying. The smell is truly excruciating!

I look over to my captain to see his reaction to this situation and glean from his experience what we should do. Captain Rick is a good man; he can be a bit intimidating because of his six-foot-three stature, his big loud voice, and his tendency to explode in anger, mostly when someone does something that he deems stupid or anytime the University of Kentucky basketball team is losing. But after working with Captain Rick for the past two years, I have seen that underneath the intimidating exterior is a warm, compassionate, empathetic person that cares about the people that he serves. But in this instance, I can see from the frown on his face, and the vein bulging across his forehead, that this was not going to be one of those compassionately empathetic moments.

As the woman lies there on the floor, Captain Rick turns to the older woman that escorted us through the house, and with his eyes squinting from the burn of the smell, and barely opening his mouth, so as not to breath in deeply, Captain Rick asks, "What is going on here?"

So the mother begins, "Well, my daughter came downstairs into the kitchen Sunday morning to eat breakfast and she slipped and fell. I tried to help her up, but couldn't, and she told me to just leave her on the floor for a little while until she got her strength to get up."

Remember, I told you about Captain Rick's tendency to explode in anger, mostly when someone does something that he deems stupid; this just happens to be one of those such times. Captain Rick interrupts the mother, "You mean to tell me she has been lying on this floor since Sunday!"

The mother nods her head in embarrassment. Captain Rick continues, "Today is Thursday--you mean to tell me, you let your daughter lie on the damn floor for five days! How come you didn't call for help!"

"I wanted to call, but my daughter didn't want me to. She was too embarrassed, so she wouldn't let me," the mother explains with shame tears falling from her eyes.

Captain Rick officially loses it. "She wouldn't let you? She's on the damn floor, how could she stop you? And what? Did you just keep feeding her?!"

The mother sheepishly answers, "She kept getting hungry. I can't let her starve to death. She's my daughter. I love her."

There it is again, the warped description of "love." And with that statement, Captain Rick articulates a plan of action. "Michael, go to the truck and retrieve two shovels, a tarp, a box of medical gloves, and some white sheets and towels from the ambulance."

I am sincerely glad to be sent out of the house into some fresh air--I mean, to the truck to retrieve some tools and supplies. I return with the supplies and we all put on two pairs each of medical gloves. Sergeant Steve and I use the two shovels to scrape up the wet messy sludge surrounding the patient as she lies quietly. After removing most of the slop from around the patient and pitching it in the kitchen garbage can, the two EMS workers and the three Engine 10 members all surround the patient to first lift her to a sitting position.

As we begin to lift her head and back from the floor to a sitting position, the patient begins to scream in agony. Because she has lain on her back for five days, she is stiff as a board, and it takes three of us to lift her head and torso upward. When we lift her upward, we finally visually understand why the stench is so horrendous. The woman has open sores all over the lower region of her back and buttocks, with small maggots eating the exposed flesh of her buttocks and upper thighs. It is a terribly disturbing sight. Every one of us can hardly contain our lunch!

Paramedic Mot cannot restrain himself; he vomits into his hand as he exits the backdoor into the back yard. Captain Rick, not wanting to let Paramedic Mot off the hook, shouts, "Mot when you're finished get back in here and help!" I think we are all felling some disgust with Paramedic Mot; we blame him for calling us. We understand that he needed us, but that doesn't make us any less agitated. I think back, only a few moments ago, back at the station, I was happy to be called on to respond to this incident because it got me out of having to do the dishes. Oh, how I would love to be at the station doing dishes, scrubbing floors, cleaning toilets, eating worms, or chewing rocks rather than in this house at this moment.

All of a sudden, the woman on the floor now begins to cry. Sobbing, she says to us, "I'm sorry, I'm sorry."

Then she screams some more as we begin to maneuver her body in order to work the sheets and towels beneath her. Captain Rick decides that it would be easier and closer to bring the ambulance to the alley in the rear rather than to try and haul the patient through the house and out the front yard. So, he orders sergeant Steven to bring the ambulance to the rear and bring the stretcher to the back door of the house. Captain Rick looks at the naked woman, who is at least now wrapped with four white sheets, and asks her a question that seems entirely unprofessional, but one that everyone wants to know.

"How big are you? How much do you weigh?"

The room seems to come to a hush; all of our inquiring minds would like to know. The patient answers, "I don't know, I mean, I'm not sure." Cap asks for an estimate. So she says, "I think I'm about 250 pounds."

Captain Rick yells, "You are not 250 pounds!"

Cap's line of questioning has a purpose; he understands that the stretcher is only rated to hold a limited amount of weight. He says out loud, "She is at least 400 pounds." He calls to Paramedic Mot, who is actually standing outside the house, and asks how much weight the stretcher is rated to hold. Mot looks down at the label on the stretcher. The label declares that the rated maximum weight is 450 pounds. Captain Rick then instructs all of us to pick the patient up, just enough to slide the tarp underneath her. Once we have her positioned lying flat on top of the the tarp, all six of us grab a portion and begin to drag her toward the door. Once at the door, we all have to muscle her down the back porch stairs that lead down to the stretcher that is sitting in the yard. We are a bit snippy with each other, but that's to be expected due to the smell and visual trauma that we're experiencing. On the count of three, we all lift with one last upward heave and gently place the patient on the stretcher. All of us let out a collective sigh of relief. But after just a few seconds, the stretcher comes crashing down to the ground. The stretcher's legs buckle under the patient's weight. Well, I guess we know she weighs more than 450 pounds. I have never seen a stretcher fall like that before.

We immediately surround the patient, checking to see if she has been injured any further. She is fine. We still use the stretcher base to roll the patient to the ambulance, but we can't use the stretcher to lift the patient into truck. So we again all have to use the points on the tarp and pull the patient into the ambulance. Paramedic Mot quickly jumps into the ambulance driver's seat, to keep from having to ride in the back with the patient. So the other paramedic sits down next to the patient in the back of the ambulance. I carefully remove my medical gloves and throw them into the small trash can on the truck. I then exit the rear of the truck, closing the double doors behind me. About three seconds later, both of the double rear doors come dramatically swinging open. It's the paramedic. He shouts, "Don't shut these doors!"

I give a small "better him than me" chuckle and walk away. This was the first and last time I have ever seen the ambulance travel to the hospital with the rear doors open.

As the ambulance pulls away the mother shouts out to her daughter, who is sitting on the floor of an ambulance, "Momma loves you!"

I walk away with my nose turned up, and this time it's not because of the ghastly odor but because of the appalling mother. This mother's "love" allowed her thirty-year-old daughter to lie in the kitchen floor in a pile of human manure for five days, while she cooked her breakfast, lunch and dinner in the same room. This is not a healthy "love"! Healthy "love" is honest, bold, and with a touch of common sense. Healthy "love" would not have fed the daughter to extreme obesity, it would not have allowed her to be eaten alive by maggots because of embarrassment. Healthy "love" would have had the courage to immediately call for help.

{LESSON 14} "Healthy "love" heals, it encourages the demoralized, uplifts the depressed, and causes the defeated to rise above and persevere through difficult moments and seasons."

CHAPTER 11
Anatomy

During our six months at the Training Academy, the fire instructors spent substantial time teaching the recruits emergency care and transportation of the sick and injured. One of the most important lessons was the section on "The Human Body." The listed objectives of this section were for the recruits to be able to identify the anatomy of the human body and to be able to identify and describe the functions of the major systems in the body, including: respiratory, circulatory, musculoskeletal, nervous, and endocrine systems. The recruits were to have a basic understanding of their role as a first responder EMT, to provide urgent response, assessment, airway management, cardiac and wound treatment, and overall patient care and transport of the sick and injured in our community. We were taught the most advanced emergency medical techniques of that day and trained to utilize the most up-to-date emergency medical tools and equipment. Though our instructors brilliantly instructed us by the book, nothing could have sufficiently prepared us for the the genuine anatomy we would see on the streets of Louisville. I mean, how real can a picture be? I know they say a picture is worth a thousand words, but a picture of CPR being performed doesn't compare to when you are pressing down onto the chest of an actual living, breathing person, and their ribs are breaking under the pressure of your hands. Well, I guess they are not actually living and breathing, that's why we're doing CPR, but you understand my point. The anatomy section shows the picture of a woman having a baby, and there is a little patch of pubic hair, and a baby coming smoothly through the vaginal canal; there is no blood, water, gooey white fluid, or poop squeezing out of her butt. I am grateful to my Academy instructors for all that they taught my recruit class about treating the human body, but nothing could prepare me for the authentic, graphic sights, sounds, and smells that we would encounter over the next twenty-three years.

In my fifth year on the Louisville Fire Department, I am a firefighter at Quint Company 9. I remember being warned during recruit school at the Fire Academy that we all need to be careful during our fifth to tenth years--that these were some of a firefighter's most dangerous years, because these were the years when firefighters think they know everything and have seen it all, and they can become complacent. They can develop tunnel vision, losing sight of the big picture or the details and the overall picture of an emergency scene. This tunnel vision can cause the firefighter to be surprised and caught off guard by new or shifting circumstances in emergency situations.

In my fifth year, I am developing some tunnel vision. I am losing my good healthy fear of fire ground situations, and since I have been an Emergency Medical Technician (EMT) for nearly six years, being a member of an ambulance crew for three years, I am starting to believe that I have seen it all. "BUUMMM! BUMMM!" The Buzzer sounds and it's a call for

Med Unit 14--that's me. Paramedic Thermis jumps into the driver's seat, and I into the passenger seat; the Quint 9 bay door lifts upward, and we are off. We are being dispatched to a motor vehicle accident on I-264 Watterson Expressway. The only details given is that there will be multiple vehicles involved, including an eighteen-wheel semi truck.

It's a beautifully hot summer afternoon in Louisville; Thermis and I are cruising down the expressway with sunglasses on our faces, some bumping radio music in the background, the siren is blaring, and we are dodging through the early mid-day traffic. I am not particularly concerned about the incident that we are responding to, because between Thermis' fifteen years as a paramedic and my extensive five years' worth of experience, my tunnel vision believes that we have seen every scenario a motor vehicle accident could offer.

As we arrive, I can see that Engine 10 and Truck 8 companies have already arrived on the scene. My quick mental size-up reveals that there are three vehicles involved (two cars and a semi truck), damage looks to be very minimal, no reports of rescue required, no overturned or crushed vehicles, looks like a negligible amount of spilled fuel that two Truck 8 members are mitigating. Just like I was thinking, no big deal, merely the typical motor vehicle accident that I had been responding to for the previous five years. Truck 8, utilizing their apparatus, has shielded most of the working scene from the oncoming I-264 traffic. Thermis pulls in front of Truck 8 and reverses the ambulance to travel backward on the left-hand side of Truck 8 in order to get closer to any possible patients.

I pick up the in-vehicle transceiver and report, "Med 14 is on the scene."

Thermis turns the siren off and places the vehicle in park. I open my door, and before I have an opportunity to step out of the vehicle, my old Sergeant Jarry from Engine 10 is standing at the door with a dumb, goofy smile on his face. As he opens my door, he speaks in his usual very high-pitched country-twanged voice, "Hey Ford, I found his foot!" Sergeant Jarry reaches into the vehicle, holding a man's detached, bare, five-toed foot, cut off at the ankle, and thrusts it into my face!

{Remember} "In general, firefighters have a warped, sometimes twisted, often times inappropriate and non-politically correct sense of humor. We beg your forgiveness."

He drops the foot into my hands (thank God, I had already donned my latex medical hand gloves.) I am immediately freaked out, and I realize then that this will not be a simple or normal motor vehicle accident. I mean, no one has ever handed me a man's detached bare foot before. Thermis and I exit the vehicle and move swiftly to the point of the accident to find and access our apparent patient. What we find is definitely something that I have never seen in my five years on the department. There is the man with the missing foot, still smashed between the rear of one car and the front bumper of another car, and he is still alive. There are so many questions racing through my mind. I am trying to mentally put together this puzzle of how this man got smashed in between two vehicles on the expressway, and how did his foot become detached, and how is he still alive? There were witnesses that later came forward who saw what took place. According to the witnesses, the victim's vehicle (vehicle #1) stalled (stopped) in the middle of the expressway, and the man exited his vehicle.

Going to the rear, he decided to try and push his vehicle from the middle to the side of the expressway. As he started to push, car #2 traveling nearly 65 MPH came barreling behind vehicle #1, but fortunately was able to come to a screeching stop directly behind the victim. Unfortunately, the 18-wheeler semi truck (vehicle #3) that was behind vehicle #2 could not stop in time and crashed into vehicle #2, which in turn smashed into vehicle #1, pinning the victim in between. When Engine 10 and Truck 8 arrived, they found the man pinned between the two vehicles. They began patient assessment on the victim and found that the man was actually severed in half. From his waistline down, he was being held together only by strings of skin and flesh.

The firefighters had made the wise decision not to move the two vehicles, because the pressure of the two vehicles smashed against the man's body was the only reason that the man had not completely bled out. Thermis' paramedic experience kicks in, which is great, because I am at a complete loss for what to do. While in the Academy, I don't remember covering what to do with a man cut in half. Those of us that know Thermis know that we affectionately called him "Therm the Worm," because of how slowly and methodically he thought, moved, and spoke. But most of us also never mistook Thermis' slow methodical movement for a lack of intelligence. At a time when most firefighters' highest level of education was a high school diploma, Thermis had a bachelor's degree in biology; he was fluent in three languages and probably could have been a doctor.

Thermis calmly begins giving instructions to the fire personnel. He instructs us to stabilize the patient with c-collar and KED (Kendrick Extrication Device) to control the bleeding coming from the patient's upper extremities, and to manage the patient's airway with a breathing mask and oxygen. The patient never speaks a word, he never really makes a sound; he just stares up at me. As I look back at him, I see the face of hopelessness; it is a disturbing face that I hope to never see again, and yet I have never been able to rid it from my mind. If I were an eye reader, I would think he was trying to tell us the pain that he was feeling, and the fear that he was experiencing. I'm sure he was thinking about his family and understanding that he was never going to see them again.

Before we start each task, Thermis looks the man in the eyes and calmly explains what we are about to do. Finally, Thermis gives permission for vehicle #2 to be moved. When vehicle # 2 is slowly removed from the man's body, we lay the man onto a backboard. As we move him, the patient's lower extremities, which are hanging by skin and shreds of flesh, fall to the ground. The patient's intestines can be seen protruding from his body. His left hand is attached to his arm only by some thin strands of skin and flesh. The patient is in complete shock, but he stares and looks at all that is going on. I recognize that there is no chance that this man will survive, but this is where firefighters especially shine brightly. Everyone understands that this man has about a zero chance of survival, and yet, every firefighter works passionately, as if the patient is their own family member. They complete each task with precision. And just like they would want the best, most competent and professional care for their own family member, that is exactly what they provide to these patients that they have never met.

We quickly place the man on the backboard, and Thermis begins placing the MAS Trousers (Military Anti-Shock trousers) on the patient, applying the garment to increase the peripheral resistance to blood flow and increase venous return to the heart. This is to decrease the blood flow out of the man's body and increase the blood flow to the vital organs that required it. We stabilized the man and prepared him for transport. One of the Engine 10 firefighters drives the ambulance to the trauma emergency hospital. Paramedic Thermis and I continue treating our patient in the back of the ambulance. Thermis injects the man with medicines and fluids, and peacefully talks to the man the entire ride to the hospital. The patient just gazes up at us, without saying one word.

When we arrive to the hospital, the doctor's and nurses are expecting and preparing for our arrival. Everyone assists with rushing the patient into "Room 9," the critical care unit. After the patient is transferred from the ambulance stretcher onto the emergency room bed, the man is immediately engulfed by a swarm of nurses and physicians. I do what I normally do when we bring a patient into Room 9--I back up into the rear-most section of the large room, and I just watch these professionals work. Unfortunately, in this case, the patient expires the moment he is laid on the hospital bed. I could not help but think about how this man literally cut his life short because of a bone-head decision to try and push his car across the expressway. At the time, I consider this to be the most ill-advised action I have ever seen. But since then, I have seen hundreds of bone-head, ill-advised actions that have injured or killed individuals. It's crazy how people can live such an intelligent, well-advised, prudent life, but have these careless lapses in their good judgment.

{LESSON 15} *"Do yourself and your family a massive favor; think carefully before you allow some rash, foolish decision to cut your life in half. Don't you be a Pusher!'"*

Speaking of "Pushers," let me tell you about the bet that led to one of the most fascinating days of my career. When I was in elementary school, I had a close friend, whose name was Kimberly. Kimberly and I would often talk about what we wanted to do and be when we grew up. I would tell Kim that I wanted to help people, I wanted to be the president and the governor, I wanted to travel to other planets, I wanted to be a football player, and I wanted to deliver babies. For some reason the one thing that Kimberly thought was just too far-fetched was me delivering a baby! She had no problem with me becoming the president, the governor, and a football player, and traveling to other planets, but delivering a baby was pushing it too far.

So, like most elementary-grade boys, I had a problem with this girl having a problem with my dream, so I guaranteed her, "I betcha that one day I will deliver a baby!" And to really make her mad I said, "I'm probably going to deliver your baby when you grow up!"

Of course her reply was, "I betcha you won't!"

Me: "I betcha I will!"

This went on back and forth for a few minutes. Amazingly, we stayed friends after this earth-shattering argument, but I never forgot about the bet that we made. After I made this declaration, I actually wondered how it would come to fruition, because I had no intention of becoming a nurse or a doctor. As

I passed through middle school and high school, my optimism for accomplishing this goal was diminishing and nearly faded from memory. But one day as I sat in the fire training academy, the EMT instructor directed the class to the EMT medical manual section on "Childbirth and Related Emergencies." Yes It had never occurred to me that firefighters deliver babies! *Oh my God! I will deliver a baby!* I'm thinking as I silently day-dream away in my seat. This section of our medical book takes on a special interest to me, so I studied this chapter more intensely, learning about the uterus, fetus, placenta, vagina or birth canal, dilation, expulsion, crowning, delivery techniques, and newborn care. So, when I graduate from the Academy, I just assume that I will be delivering babies left and right, but that isn't the case. Oh, I respond to many pregnancy incidents, but either the mother isn't ready to deliver, the baby isn't ready to be delivered, or we arrive too late, or the ambulance crew gets there in time to handle the incident.

So, after twelve years, I haven't delivered one baby. Over the years I have accomplished everything else that I said I would. I have been the president and governor (executive manager) of a number of companies and non-profit organizations, I was a good high school football player, I became a [14]"Trekkie," traveling to strange new worlds and galaxies aboard the Starships *Enterprise* and *Voyager* with every new TV episode, and during my time as a firefighter I have certainly helped a great many people. But, no baby! Until my second year serving as company commander with the rank of captain, when I am detailed in to ride in-charge of Engine Company 16. We have just finished lunch, and I am lounging on the couch in the TV room when the knock-out horn goes off, calling for

---

14   (Gene Roddenberry, 1987-1994)

Engine 16 to respond to a woman nine months pregnant and in labor. You would think that I would be excited--maybe today I will prove Lil Miss Kimberly wrong, but the truth is, at this point, I have started to believe what Kim predicted. That's so crazy! Why do we believe and hold on to the negative words and suggestions that people say about us? Maybe it's because we play those simple, seemingly insignificant words over and over in our minds, day after day, year after year, until we internalize them.

{LESSON 16} "We must surround ourselves with positive, uplifting friends, family, co-workers, and fellow students, who will fill our minds and atmosphere with words of inspiration and affirmation."

We arrive to a huge, family-oriented apartment complex called Park Hill. The three Engine 16 members and I enter the apartment on the first floor and find nearly twenty-five women, men, and children congregating in the large living room area. The expecting mother is lounging on the floor, on top of about six pillows that prop her body upward. She is a beautiful woman, in her late twenties, and she is completely naked, with her breasts lying slightly against her overly expanded belly, and her two feet flat on the floor, with her legs and knees spread apart, making her private area not-so-private. She is completely exposed. The people standing around the room are dressed in some very festive and colorful foreign outfits and look as if they are dressed and waiting for some event. I am shocked that they are all in here, especially the men. And I would have asked them all to leave, but the husband is there, and I think he invited everyone.

Well, my crew and I kneel down beside her and begin to assess the patient. We find out that this will be her second child; the first child was delivered successfully, she is about thirty-nine weeks pregnant, she has been under no doctor's care, her water broke nearly two hours ago, her contractions are less than two minutes apart, and no ambulance has even been started yet, due to there being no ambulances available in the city! Oh, Lord--I think we are about to have a baby! Well the entire crew gets set up; we put on fresh gloves, gowns, and goggles. We lay down additional blankets on the floor in front of the patient, as cushioning in anticipation of a slippery baby. The patient's sister gets behind the patient and straddles her body to give her back additional support. The patient gets very tense as a strong contraction hits her body. She groans just a bit and bears back onto her sister's chest for the approximate two minutes' duration. Then she relaxes and lays her head gently beneath her sister's cheek. Within a few seconds another contraction hits; this time the mother screams out. It's the first time I have heard her voice.

Everyone in the room feels that contraction, including me. Her husband rushes over and caresses her head. Everyone in the room is nervous with anticipation. The ensemble of friends and family stand silently around the room; even the small children have stopped running around and are quiet. Oh, the baby is coming now! The lips of the vagina open, blood and fluids pour out, and the crown of the baby's head appears. The mother begins to push, and a small pile of poop comes out her back end. This whole situation is quite messy, extremely intense, and a lot on the gross side. One more intense scream and squeeze from Momma, and the baby's head pokes out completely!

Oh my God! There is a real baby inside there! is what I'm thinking, but I keep my cool; I am the captain. We turn the baby's head toward the mother's thigh. Within just a few seconds, the baby's shoulders push through. Seconds after that, the whole baby squirts out into the hands of our female firefighter. I use a rubber bulb syringe to suction mucus from the baby's nose and mouth, and instantaneously the baby gives us the thunderous cry that we have all been waiting for. And what a gloriously, bloody, messy, wonderful sight. It's a girl. No, not just a girl, she's a bonafide miracle. The quiet spectators erupt with shouts and whistles of excitement, and dances of joy. One of the older ladies strikes up a song that everyone claps to. Now I understand why everyone is there. They were invited to a celebration of life. It was just like life, messy, filled with moments of fear and expectation--exciting, beautiful, and filled with love. What an event! I only wish Little Miss Kimberly could be here to see me. The crew and I are so honored to be part of such an awesome moment.

The ambulance crew arrives in time to clamp the umbilical cord, and we call the father over to do the honor of cutting the cord. We wrap the baby in a sterile blanket and lay her on the mother's chest. Everyone in the room congratulates the dad, and there are plenty of smiles and hugs to go around for everyone, including for the fire crew. We continue assisting the ambulance crew with preparing mother and baby for transport to the hospital. As we are cleaning up the mess that we have made in the room, I cannot help feeling inspired by this family's culture of intimacy, which allowed the entire family to be in the room and experience the birth of a new member. I am especially touched by this mother, who was so willing to share this moment with her extended family, and how she delivered her child with such grit and grace. And I was also extremely impressed by the magnificence of the human body and its ability to endure such a violently beautiful delivery of life.

{LESSON 17} "Giving birth is like life itself: messy, filled with moments of fear and expectation, exciting, beautiful, and filled with love."

There was another memorable incident where the human body showed impeccable resilience. I am assigned as Sergeant to Engine Company 7 in downtown Louisville, when we are dispatched on a report of a pedestrian struck by a motor vehicle. It's a late summer afternoon and we arrive safely to the scene of the accident and find that a pick-up truck has smacked into a forty-six-year-old man as he was crossing the street. We find the pedestrian sitting on the curb. Our New Boy grabs the medical bags and the oxygen tank. Captain Desz and I approach the man, who happens to be sitting very calmly on the curb. The man is unusually calm, to the point that we are sure that he must not have been injured. When we reach the man, we are completely blown away at the sight of his injuries. The man's tibia (the shin bone and larger of the lower leg bones) and fibula (small bone in the lower leg), in his right and left legs are broken in half and have protruded through the skin. His femur (bone that extends from the pelvis to the knee, the longest and largest bone in the body) in the left leg is also broken and protruding through the skin. The man's injuries are just ghastly! But what is even more outrageous and shocking than the injuries is this man's nonchalant demeanor. He is sitting there, laid back a bit, supported by one hand, with a cigarette in the other hand, and he acts as if he is on some picnic.

I ask the man his name and the details of what happened. He tells me that his name is Ray, and that he was trying to cross the street, when this Stupid "mother funner," came out of nowhere and just hit him! We attempt to give Ray some oxygen and take his vitals while we await the ambulance to arrive, but Ray refuses any of our attempts to help him. Ray says, "Funky" that, I'm not gonna pay for that shit!" We explain that we were here just to help, but Ray says, "Help! Help? Yaw just want to help me out of my money! "Funky" that!" Now what I have not shared with you, is that Ray is obviously a homeless man. Chances are he doesn't have any money for anyone to take. So I explain to Ray that we are not after his money, but only here to help him. Ray mumbles something under his breath as he inhales and exhales a fat puff of white tobacco smoke.

I finally ask Ray, "Aren't you in pain?"

Ray responds, "Yeah, hurts like a "mother sucker!"

And yet, no screams of agony, no cries or tears for help. In fact, Ray, our patient, has refused all treatment and any transport to the hospital. I personally have never suffered a broken bone, but I have treated a number of patients with one broken extremity, and each of those patients was screaming bloody murder at the top of their lungs. But this guy, Mr. Ray, has five broken bones poking through his skin. And he is adamantly refusing treatment. I am finally extra firm with Ray and tell him that he will absolutely die if his injuries aren't immediately treated. And I ask him, "Ray, are you ready to die?"

Ray responds, "No, I don't want to die. I guess I will go with you." And with that, the firefighters begin to assess and treat the patient. We check for a distal pulse in both of his feet and check his capillary refill. As we begin splinting his lower extremities and begin moving him to get a backboard underneath his body, we realize that his hip is also broken. I am stunned and amazed at the significance of his injuries and the lack of pain emotion Ray is displaying. For his body to take this kind of beating, Ray seems almost superhuman. The ambulance crew arrives and we place Ray onto their stretcher. As we situate him into the ambulance, Ray demands that I come with him to the hospital. I look over at Captain Desz for approval, and he nods his head, telling me to go ahead and ride in the back with Ray.

Because of the significance of Ray's injuries, the hospital emergency room staff have gathered together and prepared Room 9. As we arrive, I ask Ray once more how he is doing. Ray, with his cool demeanor, says, "I hurt--but it's cool, though." Ray is by far the coolest massively injured patient that I have ever encountered. We roll him into Trauma Room 9, and it's buzzing with tremendous activity from doctors and nurses, all dressed in white and ready to receive our patient. We move the stretcher next to the bed awaiting Ray's arrival, and everyone grabs a corner piece of the sheets lying underneath Ray, and all at the same time, pick Ray up and lay him on the Room 9 bed. The paramedic reports Ray's condition and the extent of all of his injuries. I go and stand at the rear of Trauma Room 9 and just watch these expert doctors and nurses work. They connect him to the heart monitor, place him on oxygen, stick an IV needle in his arm to draw blood and to give him some much-needed fluids. They cut his clothes off, leaving him completely naked. And Ray just lies there, completely oblivious to their efforts.

One of the doctors yells, "Mr. Ray, are you in any pain?"

Ray says calmly, "Yeah, Doc, I hurt all over."

Then it happens! The nurse on the right side of Ray's bed grabs Ray's penis, clutching it tightly with her left hand, and with her right hand begins to feed six-inch, clear plastic tubing (a catheter) down the little eye of Ray's penis. Our patient, Cool Ray, lets out a long uncontrollable, horrifying scream, "OOOOOUCHH, STOP, STOP!"

Ray starts to swing his fist at anyone and everyone that he can reach. Three doctors and four nurses can hardly keep Ray from bouncing up out of the bed. After they finally get Ray strapped down and completely immobilized, the nurse continues what she had started. And for three minutes straight, Ray screams, shrieks, yells, squeals, cries like a baby, and even threatens to kill everyone in the room, until that nurse has finished piping all six inches down Ray's most private part.

Folks, that puts everything in perspective for me. You crash into a man with a pick-up truck, break that man's hip, and legs in six places and he remains cool as a cucumber, but cause some pain to his most private part of his anatomy, and that man will want to kill you!

Like I said in the beginning of this chapter, in recruit school we sat in an anatomy class being taught the various parts and functions of the human body. We watched a few picture slides and some diagrams, but it was a bland, sterile education and did not adequately convey nearly a portion of the many ways and times that we would see the human body in its nakedness, nor see it perform in such extraordinary and diverse fashions.

One Tuesday afternoon I am riding with Paramedic Feather on Med Unit 14. We are stationed at Quint 9 fire station when we receive a call from dispatch to a commercial building in the south end of Louisville called "Fillies"--it's near the Historic Churchill Downs race track. Dispatch reports that one of the workers is sick. Paramedic Feather sits in the driver's seat, and I am in the front passenger's seat of the ambulance. We head out the door to Fillies, a local bar with nude girls swinging on poles. Now, I have been working with Feather for a couple of years; she is a sweet, thoughtful young lady. I ask her if she has ever been to a strip club.

She responds, "No, I have never been. Have you?"

Shaking my head, I reply, "No, I have never been to anything resembling a nude bar."

Because we are a few miles away, the Engine 16 fire company is also dispatched from the Hill Street Fire Station. Feather asks me why Engine 16 was dispatched from quarters instead of the three fire companies that are much closer. I explain that Engine 12 is on another incident, and Engine 10 is conducting training. Just as I finish explaining, Engine 10 calls out on the radio, "Radio, you can cancel Engine 16, we are closer."

Then Engine 16 responds, "Engine 10, what is your location, because we are at 7th and Central, I believe we may be closer."

Engine 10 says, "You can cancel Engine 16, we are at Taylor and Berry. We are closer!"

Now I am completely amused. This is so ridiculous. I have been on this department for nearly six years at this point, and I know we never, ever argue or fight over who is going to respond to a simple sick person incident. I have seen us argue and fight to see who will respond to a structure fire incident, but a sick person, never! This arguing about which company will respond to this incident is totally about the desire for this opportunity to treat some naked female anatomy! I tell Feather that although neither of us has ever been to the strip club, apparently these guys have! Engine 16 reluctantly goes back in-service, and I'm sure the Engine 10 crew gets a good chuckle, thinking that they have won. But their celebration is premature.

Engine 12 calls out on the radio, "Engine 10, you can cancel, we are on the scene."

There is a pause, and then Engine 10 says very somberly, "Engine 10 is in-service."

And with this, I am laughing out loud before the official days of LOL. We arrive shortly after. "Med 14 is on the scene," I report to dispatch.

The members of Engine 12 have already gathered the medical bags and are making their way toward the front entrance as Feather and I exit the ambulance. We enter through the front door, and it is nearly pitch black in the place; my eyes have to adjust to the dimness, and I can hardly see. There is some slow, pulsating music playing ahead of us, and to my surprise, there are multiple stages lit up, and naked women shaking "anatomy" all over the place. The dispatch said that the sick person is a worker, so I assume that they would stop the show. But as we walk past several stages, past an assortment of gyrating "anatomy," I realize that "the show must go on!" There are only a few customers--one guy sitting at the foot of each of the stages. It's really pathetic-looking to me. I mean it's the middle of an afternoon business day, and dancing naked on stage, in front of some pitiful-looking guy holding a one-dollar bill, and a huge muscular man standing right beside them both to ensure that "One Dollar Man" only looks and doesn't touch the girl that's shaking her "anatomy."

Anyway, we come to an opening that leads to the locker room. That is where we find our sick patient. She is an attractive young lady. She is sitting on the couch bare-chested, and those Engine 12 firefighters are performing some of the most attentive, excellent patient care that I have ever seen. They laid her back on the couch to make sure she is comfortable, taking her pulse and her blood pressure, getting her phone number, and her address--for billing purposes, of course. Our patient is experiencing chest pains, so Paramedic Feather asks me to connect the heart monitor to our patient's chest. I hardly have a chance to perform my assigned task before the Engine 12 Sergeant tells me, "Stand down, New Boy, and let me handle that--I need the practice."

Paramedic Feather gives me another assignment, but I don't really hear what she is saying. For some reason, I find myself extremely distracted. It may have a little to do with the three other naked women that walk into the locker room and have come over to where we are, leaning down next to me to check on their friend. Paramedic Feather calls me. "Michael, Michael--grab the bags, and let's go."

She may have actually called me more than twice, but anyway, I eventually snap back to the business at hand. We package our patient, the naked ladies say their goodbyes to their friend and of course to all of the departing firefighters, and they graciously invite us to come back whenever we get off duty. I promise to God, I have never been back. Why do I feel like you're looking at me with those doubting Steve Harvey eyes? Anyway, as we leave the building, I have a big smile on my face--not really because of all the bouncing "anatomy" that I saw today, but because I remember what Firefighter Jason told me before I was hired into this profession: "Michael, in the fire service there are no two days alike, and each day will offer up some new experience and show you something that you have never seen before." Today is another fire service day that confirms the truth of his words.

CHAPTER 12
Courage, Duty, ~~Dedication,~~ ~~Honor,~~ Infidelity

The Fire Department's mantra is "Courage, Duty, Dedication, Honor," and when performing our service to the community, most firefighters daily live up to the standard of this calling. Some of us have certainly fallen short of this commitment in our time with our fire department family and away from our spouses and children.

I am at a fire station in the South end of Louisville. It is late afternoon and we are all hanging around the kitchen after lunch, when the doorbell rings. Firefighter Met bounces up from the table with a lot of excitement and runs to answer the door. Well, this action causes the rest of us to come to the door of the kitchen, where we wait and watch to see who will come through the front door. Firefighter Met opens the door and is greeted by a gorgeously sexy girl. I don't know what she says, but whatever it is, he grabs her with both arms, squeezing her tightly, and lays a fantastically wet kiss on the interior of her lips, and whisks her off to the back dorm, which is normally private and available. We all shriek back into the kitchen and immediately begin conversing about whether that is Met's wife or not. The majority consensus is that of course that is Met's wife. Otherwise, why would he bring this "other woman" to the fire station? Why would he bring this extremely private and intimate disloyalty to the firehouse for all of us to see? Why would he bring us into his shroud of secrecy?

Well, I would like to agree with everyone that the gorgeous babe that Firefighter Met just led to a private bedroom is actually his wife. Awkwardly, I convey the fact that I have actually encountered Firefighter Met's wife on several occasions, and I remember her to be a really sweet and personable person--she is a pretty lady, but I don't remember her being gorgeous like the lady that just walked through the door. Well, the other guys head back into the kitchen, and I make my way into the front TV room to see if I can get some study time in (I'm hoping to study the back of my eyelids), and I am really hopeful that I am wrong, and the guys are right about that girl actually being Met's wife. Nearly fifteen minutes pass with me "studying" (I am asleep), when the front firehouse doorbell rings again.

This time I bounce up and rush to answer the door, mainly because I am the newest firefighter and I am closest to the door. When I open the door, there is a young, cutely dressed woman. She skips all pleasantries and angrily asks, "Michael, where is Met?"

A huge lump enters my throat--uh-oh! This is the lady I remember; this is Met's wife! And she is here standing in front of me, asking for her husband--the husband that I now know is in the back private bedroom with a beautiful young home-wrecker, possibly having some close, intimate relations. At this moment I am extremely frustrated with myself for answering this door, but mostly at Met for placing me in this compromising situation where I now have to decide to try and lie to cover for his mess or simply point her in the right direction.

I tell her, "Met is probably sleeping. I will go get him."

Met's wife refuses to wait for me. She quickly interjects, "Never mind that--I know where he is!"

She gently pushes me to the side, and she fast walks directly through the hallway and to the back private bedroom. I run through the hallway in the opposite direction to the captain's office. I'm screaming in my mind, "Mayday, Mayday!" as I burst into the captain's office.

I explain to him in my Kevin Hart voice, "It's about to go down! Met's wife just showed up and he's in the back with his girlfriend!"

We both fast walk to the rear of the firehouse, listening for the sounds of trouble. When we turn the corner, we see Firefighter Met and his wife sitting peacefully in pleasant conversation. Apparently, Met had seen through the bedroom window his wife's car pull up and was able to expel the beauty queen through the back door before his wife could catch him in the act. I wondered what made his wife show up to his work, and how did she know that her husband would be in the back bedroom? I think she may not have caught him in the act this time, but she is obviously on his track.

Later that evening, I ask Firefighter Met why he brought that girl to the firehouse, involving all of us in his mess? He just laughs and gives me some thoughtless excuse--he was just having some fun. I ask him, "Do you think it's fun for your wife, being worried that her husband is being unfaithful? Do you think that it's fun for her, not to be able to trust the person that has taken vows to always be true and faithful to her?" I continue, "Would you think it was just fun if she was unfaithful to you? How about if you lose your wife and children over just having some fun? Firefighter Met isn't really happy with my line of questioning, and once he's had enough, he just walks away. Met's wife divorces him a few years later, because of his insistence on having his "fun."

Unfortunately, that won't be the last time that I see marital negligence in my firefighter brothers and sisters. One cold winter day in a fire station in the east part of Louisville, Firefighter Priest is detailed in from another station to work with us for the next twenty-four hours. I hear him explain to the captain that today is his third 24-hour shift in a row working at a fire station. He has worked a 24-hour shift trade, worked his own 24-hour shift, and today he will be working a 24-hour over-time shift. So he asks the captain if it would be acceptable if his wife and two young children stop by for a visit later that afternoon, after lunch? The captain agrees without hesitation; it's common practice for a firefighter's family to be able to stop by the firehouse for a few minutes' visit. So, we all go about accomplishing the morning work routine.

Around 10:30 a.m., we go grocery shopping for all of the day's meals. Around 11:00, one of the firefighters cooks everyone lunch, and while we are finishing eating that meal, Firefighter Priest's wife and two children arrive at the back door that leads to the kitchen. Firefighter Priest opens the door and greets his wife and both of his children with a massive hug and some kisses. It's always a beautiful scene to see a true husband and father love on his family, and you could tell that this family has great love and respect for one another. Well, we all sit around with Firefighter Priest's family for the usual forty-five minutes, and then we are all ready for Priest to quickly send his children away--mainly because these two children get into everything; there isn't anything that they won't touch, and they scream and holler at each other the entire time. I don't understand how my captain can bear how rowdy Priest's children are, but moments later he gets up and goes to his office, and closes the door behind him.

Firefighter Priest sits on the couch with his wife all the while their children are wreaking havoc on the entire downstairs of the firehouse. What's worse, they stay so long that when the cook has finished cooking dinner, since they were still in the house, we feel compelled to invite them to dinner. Firefighter Priest's family stay with us for over six hours. Priest's family visit situation is insensitive and inconsiderate toward all of us that work and rest in that house, but none of us can be too upset--I mean, it's a father and husband just spending some quality time with his family.

After dinner, Priest says goodbye to his family with the same massive hug and kiss that they received when they arrived. It is around 6:00 p.m., and we all pitch in to quickly get the kitchen cleaned. Afterward, we all withdraw to our private spaces in the station. I go into one of the offices and work on a target hazard project that has been assigned to me. Eventually, everyone goes to bed. By the time I realize how late it is, everyone else has gone to bed. It is 1:00 a.m. when I remember that the temperature is supposed to drop below freezing that night, so I decide to go and move my personal car into the apparatus bay, so that I won't have to thaw out my vehicle in the morning. Before I go to get my vehicle, I needed to go and open the apparatus bay door. Now I could have gone straight to the wall and pushed the garage door opening button on the wall. But we had just received garage door openers that were placed on the apparatus so that we could shut the garage doors as we were leaving out on emergency incidents. So, I go into the apparatus bay, where someone has turned out all of the lights.

I walk slowly through the dark, to the sergeant's side of the apparatus, and step up into the cab to reach for the garage opener, when I am startled by movement in the back seats of the apparatus. I quickly turn to see what is causing the noise, and I can't believe my eyes! Firefighter Priest is half naked, along with some girl who isn't the wife that just spent six hours at the firehouse with him earlier in the day. You have got to be kidding me! Priest is willing to lose the life that he had built with his wonderful wife and children for some dirty sex in the back seats of a fire truck! The worst part for me is that now, I have become part of the "firefighter's code of secrecy." This "code of secrecy" especially applies to firefighters' infidelity. Infidelity in the fire station is so taboo that no one wants to be the cause of a firefighter brother or sister losing their spouse and kids. So the "code of secrecy" means that even if you totally disapprove of the member's actions against their spouse and family, your response will be to turn your head, look the other way, ignore what you saw, and never speak about it outside the confines of other fire department members.

And I am no different; I never blew the whistle on any firefighter! In this chapter, I will partially break the code of silence, but I refuse to be party to the breaking-up of a family, so

I will try to guard the cheater's identity. Only they and other members of the department will have a clue about the unfaithful member's identity.

I had a company commander (captain) that I respected a great deal as a mentor in the profession of firefighting. It was extremely fun and exciting to be part of his fire company. But my captain had a blatant disregard, disrespect, and undervaluation for his commitment to his marriage. He also had what most cheating firefighters have, and that is a secure belief in their fellow firefighters adhering to the unwritten, never-stated "secrecy code." When I arrived at his company, I had been told of his extramarital activities. The reports were always wrapped in a joking comment about how our captain loved his other girls, but for a short while, I had not noticed this behavior myself.

One summer evening, it is my day to drive the apparatus, and we are returning from a small trash fire in the nearby park. It is a picturesque day in the park, and the park is packed with people just hanging out. This is usually a great time for firefighters to shine and show off their skill, and for a great sum of them, a time to showcase their muscular, toned bodies and get lots of sexual attention from adoring female and in some case male citizens (fans). This day would be the same sort of sexually charged exchange.

As we drive parade slow through the park, the ladies begin to cry out like construction workers as we pass by, "Hey Mr. Firemen, I'm burning, come put my fire out!" "Hey firemen, come show me your big fire hose!" With our windows rolled down, we all give our parade wave to the adoring fans. We pass by a group of ladies, where one very big woman screams at the captain, "Hey cutie, come getch-you some of this!" as she slides both of her hands over her entire body in a sensual gesture.

Cap says to me, "Ford, stop the truck." But I think he's playing, so I keep going. He shouts, "Ford, stop the truck!" so I stop.

Cap then opens the door, leaps from the vehicle, and starts jogging back to the big woman who challenged him to come and get him some. The other two firefighters and I turn and poke our heads out to see what Cap is going to go do. When he reaches the woman, who is surrounded by a large crowd of women, he wraps both arms around the woman's body, grabs her very close, salsa dips her body, and lays a big fat, juicy kiss on her lips, complete with plenty of tongue to match. Then he brings her back upright, smiles, and asks the woman for a cigarette. She hands him the cigarette, lights it for him, and he comes trotting back to the fire truck with the cigarette dangling from the corner of his mouth and a very proud look on his face. We all get a very big laugh out of the whole situation.

{LESSON 18} "Unfortunately, in the heat of temptatious moments, one rarely considers the adverse effects to others, nor considers the possible consequences."

I would like to tell you that this was the worst of my captain's cheating behavior, but our company members and I had witnessed much more egregious and adulterous behavior. The reason we were witness to the behavior was because it was always directly in our faces; he never attempted to hide it. We were introduced to so many of his lady friends that we could not tell you what his actual wife looked like. This "secrecy code" is so strong that the adulterous firefighter is able to flaunt the illicit relationship in front of everyone at the fire station without any fear or trepidation of being condemned or found out.

I worked with another married firefighter, who had a woman to come spend hours with him each of his duty days for the twelve years that I knew him. She wasn't his wife, but everyone called her his "firehouse wife."

You know, I have seen some really great firefighter husbands and wives fall to the temptation of some new, fresh, hot thing, and before they know it, they're caught up in a tangled web of lies and deceit that eventually causes them to lose the people that they had forgotten were actually the most important people in their lives.

I too have fallen to temptation. I remember it vividly, because it affected me so profoundly. It was the first Saturday in May! Every Kentuckian knows what holiday is the first Saturday in May. That's Kentucky Derby Day! Growing up, I thought that day was a national holiday. The first Saturday in May is when the eyes of the world are on the great Bluegrass State of Kentucky, and specifically on the city of Louisville. That weekend really is a three-day massive party, when nearly two hundred thousand visitors come to the city to celebrate, "Derby City" style. Well, there are so many people in the streets having a grand time, that this is a perfect opportunity for firefighters to get in some "ramp time" (sitting outside on the front driveway of the fire station).

After lunch, both the engine and the truck company

members bring out some chairs to the front ramp and just hang out and watch the people riding and walking by, specifically the pretty girls. Of course, we are looking pretty good ourselves in our uniforms of the day and garnering plenty of female attention from the passing vehicles. We are all having a good time, when two new SUVs pull into the driveway. Ten of some of the most stunningly sexy college girls step out of the vehicles. Then the beauties sashay over to our group of ten firefighters, and each girl grabs the fireman of her choice. They explain that they stopped by to have some fun with some sexy firefighters. I think we all understood what kind of fun the girls were referencing. Now five of us firefighters are married and five of us are not, but you could not tell from our reactions which five are which. The girls flirt around for a few minutes and then decide that they want to take a picture with us.

That's when it happens--I know I should just go back into the firehouse, but unfortunately, in the heat of temptatious moments, one rarely considers the adverse affects to others, nor considers the possible consequences. The girl that I am paired with asks me to sit down so that she can sit on my lap to take the picture. Because of her sweet voice, and cute face, and sexy body, I comply with her request. And as we all squeeze in close to take the picture, she grabs my arm to make sure that it is wrapped around her waist for the picture. The girls laugh and smile and give us a farewell hug, and even promise to drop by later that night. When they have fully departed, we all laugh and give each other high-fives to celebrate our apparent victory. But even as I smile and slap a couple of high-fives, in my heart I am truly convicted. At this point, I have been married to my high school sweetheart for five years. In those five years, I have never given in to any advance of another woman.

In that moment, after that girl left, I begin to think about my wife, and how my wife would feel if she saw me with some girl on my lap, and my arms wrapped around that girl's waist. I thought about how I would feel, if I saw my wife sitting on another man's lap, and his arms wrapped around her waist. That thought makes me sick to my stomach. Some of you may be thinking I'm blowing this way out of proportion, because this was small and insignificant. But the truth is, these work-place flings, affairs, and sexual encounters start with some small flirting, some playful touching, or some intimate con-versations. I make a decision that day, that I don't want to be one of those people that lives a double life as a firefighter of honor, bravery, commitment, and honesty and then also be a lying, cheating, deceitful, dishonest, disloyal husband and father. After counting up the cost, I decide that losing my wife, family, and self-respect for some hot new temptation is too high a cost. From that day forward, I decide that not only will I strive to be faithful to my wife, but that I will also strive to be an advocate for healthy marriages among all firefight-ers, because ultimately, a healthy home life makes a healthier firefighter.

Through the years, I have had multiple opportunities to fulfil this commitment of supporting and encouraging fire-fighters to pursue and guard the health of their marriages. There was no time more evident of this effort than in 2002, when a Louisville Engine Company was forced to close down due to required emergency repairs. The fire crew had to move-into our Truck and Engine Fire station for six months. For those six months there was a total of sixteen fire personnel on duty each day. It was one gigantic slumber party--every-one genuinely enjoyed the camaraderie, not to mention the testosterone levels were off the charts! There was plenty of wrestling, playful pushing and shoving, practical jokes, and sexually charged conversations.

One particular evening, I walk into the sergeant's office to find about eight firemen lounging around the room in deep discussion. The room is tiny; it's about the size of a large residential walk-in closet. There are two couches facing each other, and three office chairs. I stand up against the corner wall and listen to the men go around the room, each griping and complaining, and laying some serious charges against their wives. As the room swirls with marital complaints, the guys are becoming frenzied with wild, sometimes bitter criticisms of their spouses.

One firefighter complains, "When I come home, my wife immediately pushes the kids in my face and wants me to take them outside to play, or she has some chore that she wants me to do. She doesn't consider the fact that I have been here at work for 24 hours, and when I get home I'm tired or just need a little me time before she hands me her honey-do list!"

The crowd of firefighters chime in with complete agreement. Another firefighter inserts his complaint, "My damn wife always whines about us not having enough money to pay all the bills, or go on a vacation, but then anytime I work some overtime at the firehouse or a few days at my part-time job, she then complains that I'm not home enough."

Everyone cheers in agreement at that statement. But then one of the guys adds the meanest statement: "I hate that my wife has just let herself go. I mean, she used to look good, now she just looks homely."

After this, the guys speak of being close to divorcing their wives. Now at this, I have heard enough. I speak up. "Yaw ought to be ashamed of yourselves." I begin to tear into each one of the complaints like a lawyer tears into the false testimony of someone on the witness stand. To the argument that the firefighter has been at work for 24 hours, "Your spouse has also been at work for the same 24 hours that you worked. Maybe she worked all day at home, taking care of the house and kids, or maybe she went to work and then came home and took care of the house and kids. Have you considered the fact that she is just as tired as you are, or more? You have been so concerned about your 'me time' that you failed to consider that after she has cared for your children and whatever other issues that you were absent from during your duty day, that maybe she also requires some 'me time' of her own to help keep her sanity, and energy to perform her motherly and wifely duties and desires?"

Everyone listens and ponders in silence as I continue, "So you're mad that your wife is concerned about the finances, but aren't you concerned about the finances? Don't you want to be able to take your family on a vacation?" They all nod in agreement. I continue, "Of course! So instead of us getting upset because our spouse states their concerns, how bout we become mature husbands and develop a strategic plan with our wives to address our financial concerns and strategize how and when we will achieve our vacation and all of our family goals. And as for her expressing her anguish over us working multiple days and even multiple jobs, there is a lot for us to consider:

1. All of you should thank God that you have a wife that desires to have you home. The fire department has to pay me big money to be around you buzzards for 24

hours, and I still don't like it! I think your wives are saints for putting up with you every day!

2. If we are away from home day after day, are we really being great husbands or fathers?

3. When we are at the firehouse for 24 hours, we know our wives are sometimes lonely or even afraid while at home alone or with the children. And then we are gone sometimes two or three duty days in a row."

Firefighter Tim confesses, "You know we live in a rural area, and my wife calls me at work sometimes because she gets worried that someone might break into the house. I have to talk to her until she falls asleep."

I jump back in, "See, we are so busy thinking about ourselves, we haven't considered what our wives are enduring on behalf of our family. I had an old major named Bruce tell me that once his kids had grown up, his wife finally shared with him that for years, she had packed up herself and their children and traveled to her mother's house every night that he was on duty and rushed back home the next morning before he arrived home. All because she was afraid of being alone at night."

I tell the guys that maybe it would be more beneficial if we talked with our wives about not only our frustrations, but actually listen to their fears, frustrations, and possible considerations and solutions to dealing with all of our family issues.

Finally, we all address the attractiveness of our wives. And by this time the atmosphere in the room has been converted from the negative, self-absorbed, finger-pointing wife-bashing to a positive, solution-oriented, successful marital ideas exchange. Sometimes firefighters are approached in the public by some groupie types of women that have some sexualized fantasy of firefighters. They have seen some television show or read some girly "love" novel about some gorgeous, hypersexual firefighter that steams into their lives and sets their heart and body ablaze. These women come around flirting, and sometimes offering the firefighter more than a sexual comment and a smile! They may offer some fling or respite from what the firefighter may deem an uneventful, passionless marriage. Many firefighters allow this attention, the stature and the respect of the job and uniform to not only boost their ego, but also falsely inflate their image of themselves as compared with their view of their spouse. I have seen men that are clearly mediocre in every way, who all of a sudden believe that they are a 10 on the desirable scale.

I told one of my firefighter friends in the room, "Jug Head [his nickname], your wife is an absolute saint! I could not even begin to understand how or why she endures having your fat, hairy belly and back touch her, let alone slide over the top of her at night, and how she has the strength to allow that jug head of yours to lay on her chest! It's a wonder how she does it!"

Of course he answers with complete confidence, "That girl is the luckiest girl in the world to have me!"

Seriously, we sometimes look at our wives and see things hanging a little lower, or their faces with a few wrinkles, or their hair with some strands of gray, but have we considered that we aren't spring chickens anymore either? And if our spouse is looking a bit homely, it may be because she's not feeling beautiful. And if our wives are not feeling beautiful, then maybe we should spend more effort romancing them like we used to when we were trying to win their affections. Maybe if we become more loving and attentive husbands, we would bring out the brilliance and sparkle that we remember and so desire in our wives.

We finally end our two-hour evening discussion, and we all walk away hopeful and encouraged to become better husbands and fathers and of developing a marriage that's not on the cliff of divorce. For the next few weeks, after dinner, we all met in the same room for our uplifting conversation about marriage and life. I will never forget how so many of our marriages were in turmoil, and how many of them were saved just by connecting with others that were not swirling with negative comments and advice, but offered up positive strategies for success, and self-introspective challenges to work on our personal deficiencies.

For every firefighter that chooses to break their marital covenant, there are many more who choose to honor the love and the commitment that they have made to their spouse. And I am grateful to have served with and to have been surrounded by such a fantastic group of loyal family men that are faithful and attentive to their wives. I salute each of them, my friends Douglas, Ricky Bobby, Bruce, Zion, Mike, Clifford, Randy, William, Brian, Damon, Larry, Curtis, Melvyn, Little Bear, and many more.

CHAPTER 13
Rescue Rangers

It is a scorching July afternoon at Truck Company 4. The guys and I have just finished some in-house training, so we are lounging around slurping down on some sweet yellow banana popsicles. Without warning, the knock-out buzzer screams out! It's a report of a commercial fire alarm, with smoke and fire showing inside the metropolitan sewer plant. And from the sound of the dispatcher's voice, this is going to be a working fire. With popsicles in hand, we all race to the fire trucks. I flip off my shoes, place each leg into the already prepared bunker pants, pull the pants up and fasten the buckle, then slip the Nomax Hood over my head so that my face is the only part showing. I then reach for my fire coat that is hanging on the fire truck's door handle. I drape it around me, placing both arms in simultaneously, and moving from the bottom upward, fastening all eight buckles on the coat, ensuring to align the inside Velcro lining for maximum fire protection. Finally, I hop on the truck just as it's pulling out, all of which takes place in less than 30 seconds.

As the fire truck barrels down the streets, dodging the

afternoon traffic, I begin my mental size-up of the situation that we might find upon arrival to the scene. I have never been to this facility, but I have been to enough of these types of plants to know that there are always a good number of facility workers who may be in harm's way, who may require our rescue efforts to be deployed. Though I never wish anyone to be caught in harm's way, I can't stop the adrenaline rush and can't help but be excited about the opportunity, the necessity to implement my rescue skills. Who knows, this might be a burning inferno; the sewer plant is directly next to the oil refinery.

By the time we arrive, I have already strapped the breathing apparatus over my shoulders, and buckled the self-contained breathing apparatus (SCBA) belt around my waist, placed the fire helmet over my head and the fire gloves on my hands. Truck 4, Engine 22, Engine 19, and Battalion Chief 51 pull through the plant gates, I size up the scene, and to my surprise and disappointment, there is no smoke or fire showing, there is no mass hysteria of workers--shoot, the workers aren't even walking fast. Captain Gett turns around and looks at me, and I know that's his signal for "Let's go." So I grab my fire ax and leap into a full sprint to catch up with Captain Gett. The plant manager comes up to Captain Gett and describes the situation. He says that there is a fire in one of the product vats, and that it has spread throughout the plant because it traveled on the mechanical belt inside the vat. He also explains that the fire is completely contained within the vats. I am a little more disappointed, because I realize there won't be any rescues today.

Captain Gett releases all the other responding companies to return to regular service, except for Engine 22. He instructs them to connect to a hydrant and bring him a hose line. He then tells the plant manager to take us to the affected area. The manager fast walks us back about what feels like a mile away into a very large sewage heating and drying area. As we enter this very large room, there is an awful stench in the atmosphere. I then remember that we are in a sewage treatment plant. But I haven't ever considered what they do in this facility, and I am also beginning to wonder--what does the plant manager mean by the "product" being on fire?

The plant manager speaks up while pointing upward. "There it is--you can get to it through that scuttle hole."

I can't take it anymore. Maybe everyone else knows, but I don't. So I ask the manager, "What product is burning and why does it smell so horrendous?"

The plant manager says with a smirk, "It's dried pellets of human feces!"

My mouth just drops. "You mean there are dried poo-poo pellets on fire in those vats? Why?"

The plant manager briefly attempts to explain something about how they are used as biofuel for the reduction of carbon dioxide emission. Whatever they are used for, they stink to high heaven! I can't begin to put into words what tons of burning poop smell like, other than to just tell you that it's brutal! For some reason that I can't seem to remember, the captain of Engine 22 shows up with his sergeant instead of his new firefighter, dragging a charged hose line. Captain Gett asks whether the conveyer belts have been stopped, and if there is another entrance into the vat.

The plant manager says, "Yes, the conveyer belt is stopped,

and no, there are no other entrances. Furthermore, the only way to keep the fire from burning through--someone will need to take a fire hose and travel through the three-hundred-foot-long vat and wet down the burning product."

Burning product! I wish he would stop calling it product and call it what it is: burning poo-poo! I'll tell you what I am really nervous about. Whose job will it be to climb up into that vat and crawl through 300 feet of dried burning poo-poo pellets, and spray it all down with 250 gallons/minute of water that will revive the poo back to its original state of pure funk poo-mud! Yeah, I'm looking around as if I don't already know what's about to happen. I mean everybody standing around me, are persons of rank--two captains and a sergeant. Crap! I'm the low man on the totem pole; at this point in my career I'm a firefighter without rank. The engine sergeant puts the 18-foot straight-beam ladder in place, up against the vat door opening. My heart just sinks into my stomach. I drop the fire ax, take my SCBA pack off my shoulders and lay it on the plant floor. I walk over to Engine 22 captain and take the charged fire hose from his hands, walk to the ladder, and start my way up the rungs.

After I have taken a few steps upward, Captain Gett grabs the back of my pants and tells me to come back down. I think maybe I have forgotten something. So I come back down, and Captain Gett orders me to hand him the hose line and says, "Ford, I got this one!"

He grabs the hose line and quickly maneuvers up the ladder and into the opening of the vat where the poo-poo smoke was pouring out. Oh my God, I have been saved, I have been rescued from the burning fiery poo-poo furnace! I thought there wasn't going to be any rescues on this incident—boy, was I wrong! Little did I know that it was going to be me in need of rescuing. We all assist Captain Gett into the vat opening and feed the hose line to him as he travels further into the burning poo-poo pellets. As the rest of us stand underneath the opening, and wet rehydrated brown and black sewage begins to pour onto the ground next to us, I realize that I'm not the only person feeling thankful to be rescued from the burning fiery poo-poo furnace. Captain Gett has done what each of us loathed to do.

Captain Gett keeps constant radio contact with us as he crawls all the way through the vat. He is in that poo hole for nearly an hour. When he arrives back to the vat opening and begins to make his exit, he is completely covered from head to toe in silky wet grayish-black poo poo mud. He is nearly unbearable to look at and completely intolerable to smell. We take the fire hose and spray the big poo pieces off of Captain Gett's face, helmet, fire coat, bunker pants and boots. I don some medical gloves and assist Captain Gett with unfastening and shedding his fire coat. The plant manager tells us not to worry about cleanup, that he has a crew coming in to clean and sanitize the entire area.

Captain Gett and I take the long walk back to the fire truck. I'm not sure if Captain Gett ever completed a bio-hazard exposure report for this incident, but I will tell you this--he smelled like burnt poo-poo pellets for the next two months. I carry Captain Gett's SCBA pack and equipment back to the apparatus with a feeling of honor, having the thought that Captain Gett just did what many leaders neglect to do; Captain Gett led selflessly by example. I always had crazy respect for this man as a great firefighter and a skilled fire service instructor, but now I also appreciate him as a humble and selfless leader. Captain Gett, if you are reading this, I can't remember if I ever expressed my appreciation for you rescuing me in that situation and for all the time and effort you poured into me, but I tell you now, "Thank you, and I salute you, sir!

Serving with Captain Gett seemed to always be sort of an adventure. While part of Truck Company 4, and sometimes part of an engine company together, we were awarded a number of Unit Citation Awards for our efforts during fire emergency incidents. There was a fire in the east end of Louisville that Captain Gett, myself, and firefighter "Green Giant" (sometimes called "Green Mile") made entry into a burning massive two-story residential house. We were fully dressed in all our firefighting protective clothing and gear:

- Protective Hood – Helps protect the firefighter's neck, face, and ears from steam and radiant heat

- Protective Coat and Pants – Helps protect firefighter's torso and limbs from cuts, radiant heat, chemicals, and possesses limited flame retardant

- Fire Boots – Protect the firefighter's feet from burns, punctures, chemicals, crushing from falling heavy debris

- Fire Gloves – Protects the firefighter's hands from burns, chemicals, and injury

- Helmet – Protects the firefighter's head from falling debris and injury

- Self-contained breathing apparatus (SCBA) and mask – Protects the firefighter's face, mouth, and lungs from toxic smoke, superheated gases, and chemicals

- Personal alert safety system (PASS device) – Emits loud squawking sound that alerts others that a firefighter has remained motionless for 30 seconds and may be incapacitated or injured and requires immediate assistance

Before we enter the house, we all kneel at the door to strap our face-pieces onto our heads, turn on our breathing air, place our hands inside our gloves, and for me, say a quick prayer of protection. As we enter the burning house from the front door with our inch and ¾ fire hose line, nothing of the interior of the house can be seen. The room is in utter darkness. We can't even see our hands in front of our faces. This is normal visibility in a fire, so we push forward, searching for the seat or base of the fire and any victims that may be trapped. Though we haven't yet seen the actual flames of fire in the interior of the house, we can certainly feel the intense radiating heat bearing down on us through our protective gear and straight to our bodies. The sensation feels like your skin is boiling and your face and neck are being sun-scorched.

We press on without seeing, but feeling our way through the darkness, and following our other senses. The earsplitting noise of sirens, tools banging, gas saws roaring, fire engines running, people shouting on the outside, materials burning, and the crashing of falling ceilings and firefighters knocking furniture over as they travel through the dark is deafening! The only way to communicate with the firefighter next to you is to shout at them at the top of your voice. The heat is so severe that the three of us are forced to crawl on our hands and knees to navigate through the house and up the stairs to the second-floor landing. Once there, we are finally allowed to see, due to the bright light shining from the orange, glowing fire. The three of us are now traveling on our knees in a straight line. I am in front, because I have the fire hose nozzle. As we are crawling near the flames in the open floor area, I open the adjustable nozzle to a wide- fog water stream to give us some coverage from the radiant heat of this fire. We look like superheroes with this wide circular shield of water, until I finally adjust the water stream to shoot intermittent burst of waters straight at the wall of flames. As water crashes into the flames at 125 gallons of water per minute, the room darkens again, and the steam is just about unbearably blistering our entire bodies.

Captain Gett directs Green Giant to use his plaster hook to pull the ceilings down to check for fire extension above us. Once he pokes through the plaster ceiling, fire descends down like rain. Captain Gett realizes that there is a set of wooden stairs that lead up into the attic, so we make our way up to the attic that is completely engulfed in flames. I take the lead onto the attic floor with Captain Gett and Green Giant pulling the water filled hose up the stairs. We are surrounded by fire and begin the work of extinguishing the flames. Then, we see something unusual--a huge, orange ball of fire coming from the window. This great ball of fire looks as if it is blowing from one of those World War II-era military flamethrowers, and it is engulfing half of the room. In this moment we feel like Thanksgiving turkeys roasting in Grandma's oven, as the temperature rises well past 1,000 degrees Fahrenheit. The three of us hunker down together underneath an umbrella of water that I have spraying from my fog water nozzle. I have no idea what is causing this fireball anomaly, but Captain Gett is an experienced fire captain who knows exactly what is going on. Someone has placed an elevated master stream nozzle into the attic window that shoots out 1000 gallons of water per minute, and it is being directed straight into this attic window, causing the fire to be pushed back onto the three of us. Apparently, no one knows that the three of us have made it into the attic.

Captain Gett screams through his hand held radio, "Turn that damn water off--we are in the attic!" Within seconds, the water stops, and the fireball dissipates. We finally extinguish the fire and make our exit. There are no residents needing to be rescued that day, but I can't help but thank God for His grace that there is no need for three firefighters to be rescued.

There is also the residential house fire were Captain Gett and I have to tear open the metal, plywood, and shingle-layered gable roof of a burning two-story house for ventilation operations with an ax, because the quick-vent chainsaw wouldn't start. We stand on top of the sloped metal roof, taking turns with the ax, trying to smash through in order to properly vent the fire. After each of us has taken nearly a hundred whacks, we finally cut the square hole into the roof, and the fire and the black superheated smoke forcefully funnel through. To say that we are exhausted would be an understatement. We both just lie on the roof as if we are warming ourselves by a campfire. Our efforts certainly enable the Engine Company to make entry into the structure and effect a timely rescue of two trapped victims.

There were numerous incidents when Captain Gett led his fire crew to successful extinguishment of a fire and the rescue of endangered citizens, but there was one particular rescue that was more memorable for me. One late afternoon, around 1730 hours (that's 5:30 p.m.), the knockout buzzer reverberates throughout the station, just as we are sitting down for dinner. The dispatcher reports that there is a residential structure fire only three blocks from the fire station. Truck Company 4, Engine Company 22, Engine Company 17, and Battalion 1 are all sent on emergency through the streets of Beautiful West Louisville to this box alarm/house fire. Truck Company 4 arrives to the scene first, and I hear Captain Gett give the initial size-up: "Truck 4 and Engine 22 are on the scene at 913 Andrea Avenue, we have a two-story brick residential home; there is nothing showing." As the apparatus comes to a complete stop in front of the house, Captain Gett and I exit the truck, clothed in full turnout gear. We quick step to the front of the residence, where there is a tall, thin, neatly dressed man smiling at us as we make our way up the porch steps. Captain Gett asks the gentleman if there is a fire.

The thin man in the pink shirt and tight white pants looks at all of the fire trucks, flashing lights, and the arriving firefighters, and answers, "Wow, now this is service! Mr. Officer, I called because I'm locked out of my house, and I think I left the stove on, and my cat may be in danger."

Captain Gett keys the microphone on the radio and reports to the battalion chief that there is no fire, possibly food on the stove, and that Truck 4 and Engine 22 can handle the situation. And with that, all the other units go back into service. Captain Gett tells me to go and get a ladder so that we can check and see if any of the second-floor windows are unlocked. Another firefighter and I bring back an 18-foot ladder, place it against the side of the house, and make entry into the house from an unlocked window. When we get inside the residence, we proceed to the kitchen first, only to find that the stove not only isn't on, there is no food near the stove, and I never see a cat. We go to unlock the front door, where Captain Gett and the thin gentleman are waiting and let them inside. We report to Cap, that we have found the stove off and no food cooking.

The thin gentleman just smiles and says, "I'm so sorry, Mr. Officer; I thought I left the stove on."

And with that said, we leave, and Captain Gett places us back in service.

The next week, late one afternoon, around 1730 hours (that's 5:30 p.m.), the knockout buzzer reverberates throughout the station, just as we are sitting down for dinner. The dispatcher reports that there is a residential structure fire only three blocks from the fire station. Truck Company 4, Engine Company 22, Engine Company 17, and Battalion 1 are all sent on emergency through the streets of Beautiful West Louisville to this box alarm/house fire. Truck Company 4 arrives to the scene first, and I hear Captain Gett give the initial size-up: "Truck 4 and Engine 22 are on the scene at 913 Andrea Avenue, we have a two-story brick residential home; there is nothing showing."

As the apparatus comes to a complete stop in front of the house, Captain Gett and I exit the truck clothed in full turnout gear. We quick-step to the front of the residence, where there is the same, tall, thin, neatly dressed man we met last week, smiling at us as we make our way up the porch steps. Captain Gett asks the gentleman if there is a fire. The thin man, dressed in a gorgeous lavender blouse and a pair of dark purple jeans, looking at all of the fire trucks, flashing lights, and the arriving firefighters, answers, "Mr. Officer, it's you again. Well, I called because I'm locked out of my house again, and I left some food cooking on the stove, and I was scared that I would burn the house down, and my dog may be in danger!"

Captain Gett keys the microphone on the radio and reports to the Battalion Chief that there is no fire, possibly food on the stove, and that Truck 4 and Engine 22 can handle the situation. And with that, all the other units go back into service. Captain Gett tells me to go and get a ladder so that we can check and see if any of the second-floor windows are unlocked. Another firefighter and I bring back an 18-foot ladder, place it against the side of the house, and make entry into the house from an unlocked window. When we get inside the residence, we proceed to the kitchen first; this time there is a pot of water boiling on the stove, but no food of any kind around the stove, and I never see any dog.

We go to unlock the front door, where Captain Gett and the thin gentleman are waiting, and let them inside. We report to Cap, that we have found water boiling on the stove. The thin gentleman smiles and says, "I'm so sorry, Mr. Officer. I'm going to have to invite you boys over for dinner one day."

And with that said, we leave, and Captain Gett places us back in service.

The next week, late one afternoon, around 1730 hours (that's 5:30 p.m.), the knockout buzzer reverberates throughout the station, just as we are sitting down for dinner. The dispatcher reports that there is a residential structure fire only three blocks from the fire station. Truck Company 4, Engine Company 22, Engine Company 17, and Battalion 1 are all sent on emergency through the streets of Beautiful West Louisville to this box alarm/house fire. Truck Company 4 arrives to the scene first, and I hear Captain Gett give the initial size-up:

"Truck 4 and Engine 22 are on the scene at 913 Andrea Avenue, we have a two-story brick residential home. There is nothing showing!" Then Cap adds, "Truck 4 can handle OK, all other responding companies can return to service."

As the apparatus comes to a complete stop in front of the house, Captain Gett and I exit the truck clothed in full turnout gear. We quick-step to the front of the residence, where the tall, thin, neatly dressed man is standing smiling at us as we make our way up the porch steps. Captain Gett asks the gentleman if there is a fire. The thin man, dressed in a flower-printed top and bottom short set, says in a fake distressed voice, "Mr. Officer, I called because I'm locked out of my house, and I left the stove on, and my puppy is trapped in the house! He needs to be rescued! Please Mr. Officer, save my puppy!"

The other firefighter and I get ready to go and retrieve the ladder as we had done the two previous times before, but Captain Gett shouts at us, "Wait! This man's puppy is in immediate danger--we need to get in the house now and rescue this little dog! We don't have time for a ladder!"

And without warning, Captain Gett rears back, and slams his big 12-inch fire boot into the door. With one kick, the entire door comes crashing down, frame and all! The smirk that was on the gentleman's face now matches the surprised expression that the other firefighter and I have on our faces. Captain Gett tells the man, "There, your puppy is saved!"

And with that, the puppy is rescued, though I never see any puppy. Captain Gett gives us a nod, and we follow him off the porch and back to the truck. Captain Gett places Truck 4 back in service, and—guess what? That fine thin gentleman never requires our rescue assistance again.

My most miserable day on the department came so un-expectedly and without warning. I am in my third year. Firefighter Joe, one of my classmates from drill school, calls and asks me to come work a trade for him over at Truck 9. I am just leaving my 24-hour shift over at Engine 10, where we have been up without rest for most of the night, fighting a house fire and conducting overhaul operations through the night. I am extremely tired, but I think, *Truck 9 is one of the slowest fire stations in the department; what could happen?* I think I will just show up and do a little housework, then sneak off and get me a quick siesta right after lunch. I show up that morning to Truck 9, place my gear on the truck, and report to Captain Dridge so that he can give me my assign-ments. Captain Dridge brings the Truck 9 members together for morning roll-call and apparently has been quite displeased with his crew's effort the past few duty days. So he informs the crew, "No more Mr. Nice Guy!" He tells me, "Sorry, Mr. Ford, but today you are Firefighter Joe, and he is part of the prob-lem, so you will have to suffer for him."

I don't know what that means, but I'm really not happy with my buddy Joe; I have a feeling that he knew this was coming and that's why he made this trade. Well, we get start-ed. I complete my morning assignments:

1. Clean and sanitize six urinals, seven toilets, ten sinks, three shower rooms, three locker rooms, two massive bedrooms, two offices, and mopped eleven rooms.

2. Assist the sergeant with checking and conducting maintenance on three fire trucks, along with the power saws, ladders, and tools.

3. Join the crew in mowing the two-acre lawn

By the time we finish mowing, it's noon and I am worn-out. I was so right about it being a slow house; I'm really wishing for the bell to ring, and for some fire incident to come in and save us from all this cleaning. Captain Dridge gathers us all up and tells us to get cleaned up so that we can go to the store and get groceries for lunch and dinner. I'm thinking, *Yes! We finally get a break, and I was starving anyway. I hope these guys at Truck 9 can cook!* Captain Dridge continues, "Ford, it was Joe's day to cook, so you're it--and make sure it's good."

I nod and say, "Yes, sir," signifying that I understand, but in my mind I'm really aggravated with my buddy Joe. He knew that it was his day to cook. We head to the store and I think about what I am going to whip up for these guys. I collect five dollars from all eight members, so I have forty dollars total to come up with lunch and dinner. I'm a slow, but thrifty shopper, diligently harvesting each required ingredient for my "Legendary Italian Chicken Pasta Salad" for lunch, and my "Famous Mushroom and Swiss Firehouse Burgers" for dinner. After we return from the store, while the guys are given further assignments, repainting the company colors onto each tool on the apparatus, I go to work in the kitchen.

1. Five pounds of raw chicken breasts, diced into a pile of cubes

2. Two pounds of diced pepperonis (this is the secret flavoring)

3. Two huge yellow onions, diced

I position the massive 16-inch black iron skillet on to the gas Vulcan stove, and bring it to the temperature of piping-hot. I pour in a cup of Italian dressing, allowing it to come to a sizzle, and then the diced onions, pepperoni and a hit of Red's hot sauce. Once the pepperoni has fully discharged its natural oils, then I pour in the pile of chicken cubes. While the flavor is being infused into the chicken, I start the tedious work of chopping the fresh broccoli, cauliflower, celery, green onions and baby carrots. I then pour six boxes of rainbow swirl noodles into the boiling hot pot of water. As the noodles are coming to a perfect texture, the chicken is being encrusted with a red peppery layer of flavor. Once everything is properly prepared, I mix it all together in an enormous roasting pan, where the oils from the pepperoni and chicken meats wet the noodles and vegetables with intense savory flavoring that smacks the eater right in the mouth!

I prep the table with napkins, silverware, ranch dressing, and some shredded sharp cheddar cheese. I even have some fresh, hot baked Italian bread that I pull from the oven and slice for each person to have two pieces. Finally, around two o'clock I go to the intercom and call everyone for lunch, "Come and get it! Come and get it!"

The guys are just finishing up their tool painting, and I don't believe that they even bother to wash their hands. Everyone piles into the kitchen, and over to the stove. Each person piles the pasta deep and high into their bowls. As they sat at the table, there was no conversation, just, oohs, ahs, mms, yums, grunts, and burps. Finally, Captain Dridge puts everyone's sentiments into actual words. "Mr. Ford, you are welcome to work here at Quint 9 anytime you want. Firefighter Joe has never made us a meal like this."

"Thank you, sir," I reply.

After everyone has had their fill, we all start to wash dishes and clean up the kitchen. I'm glad that everyone enjoyed my meal, but I'm exhausted. "Legendary Italian Chicken Pasta Salad" is a labor-intensive meal. Well, it's a bit after 2:30 p.m., so as soon as we're finished cleaning the kitchen, I have got to grab me a nap before it's time to cook dinner. Captain Dridge finally gets up from the table and announces, "As soon as you guys are finished with the dishes, get your uniform shirts on and let's load up for about two hours of home inspections."

Captain Dridge can't see our faces, because he is standing in the dining area which is separated by a brick wall from the actual cooking area, but I can tell you, that we are furious, but we all respond, "Yes, sir."

Captain Dridge exits the kitchen, and all of us begin to voice our complaints about all the busy work Captain Dridge is dispensing today. I make a comment to the guys about Captain Dridge's good stamina to keep up this working pace. Everyone quickly snaps back at me, "The only reason that he isn't tired is because while we were working, he was on the couch in his office taking a nap!" Anyway, we all get dressed and load the truck with smoke detectors, red numbered department identification stickers, and plenty of dry-wall nails, and travel to the neighborhood that Captain Dridge identified. The Louisville Fire Department conducts home inspections as part of our overall fire prevention program to decrease the likelihood of residential fires. We also install free smoke detectors to any resident in the Louisville area, to ensure that every citizen has these life-saving devices. So we spend the next two hours walking the 400- house sub-division, going door-to-door, asking the residents to allow us to conduct a free fire safety inspection and to install a free smoke detector if one is needed. Have I mentioned how tired and sleepy I am? The only thing that is keeping me up right now is the constant walking up and down these hilly streets, the constant banging on these doors, and the beautifully warm, autumn sunny weather.

Around 1700 hours (5 p.m.), we install our last smoke detector device and finish our last house inspection. On the way back to the fire station, Captain Dridge looks back at me and comments, "Hey Mike, when we get back, you better get started on dinner right away before the storms come in."

I don't know anything about some storms, and don't care-- the only thing I really hear him say is, "No sleep for you!"

As soon as we get back to the station, I start on the next meal, my "Famous Mushroom and Swiss Firehouse Burgers." First, I peel about twelve stout Idaho potatoes, slicing them into long, slender wedges for some "Double Dipped Fries." I place two black iron skillets on the gas stove, over top of the bright blue flame and bring it to a light smoke. I pour the secret sauce of two full liquid packages of onion soup into the hot iron skillets. Then I form up the raw ground chuck beef into about sixteen half-pound patties, lightly seasoning them with a shaking of sea salt and ground black pepper, and strategically place them into the two iron skillets of soupy onion concoction. I cover both skillets with metal tops, to allow the reduction of the onion soup to saturate the meat with savory, juicy flavoring. While that's basting, I slice some fresh Portobello mushrooms and place them on top of each burger, just in time to bring them to a tender consistency. In the meantime, I sauté a skillet of parmesan-crusted garlic Brussels sprouts in a thin layer of olive oil. Finally, I top each burger with two slices of peppered Swiss cheese, pull up the golden brown, crispy potato wedges from their second dip in the hot cooking vegetable oil, and call the guys in to eat.

Everyone rushes into the kitchen with great anticipation of a second fantastic meal. As they all sit at the table, again there is very little discussion at first, just lots of slurping, chomping, along with plenty of oohs, ahhs, mms, yums, grunts and burps. Cooking success! Around 1830 hours (6:30 p.m.), we finish cleaning the kitchen. When I exit the kitchen, I sneak past the captain's office for fear of him handing me another assignment, but I notice that the sun has quickly been overshadowed by some nasty-looking black clouds and that it has started to rain. I rush into the bedroom to try and catch at least an hour and a half worth of sleep before it will be time for me to ride my shift on the Med 14 ambulance.

I find an empty bed, and place my sheets and comforter down, and without hesitation, I lie down and smash my face into the softness of my pillow and in seconds, I am comatose. Less than three minutes pass. I am finally, nearly asleep when the knock-out blasts, "Bumm! Bumm!"

"NOOOOO!"

Radio dispatches Quint 9 to a reported water rescue of an elderly man trapped in a flooded, residential basement. I roll out of bed, and rush over to the fire truck, grab my gear, and within a minute, the truck is out of the gate. As we speed toward the distressed man, our driver is being extra cautious because the rain is coming down so heavily that he can hardly see the vehicles in front of the truck. When we pull in front of the residence, all of us charge toward the house expecting to have to force entry. But to our surprise, an elderly man nervously greets us at the front door. He tells us to hurry because his babies are trapped in the basement, and the water is rising. Now I will admit, there are a few questions rolling through our minds:

1. The report said that the elderly man was trapped in the flooded basement, but this man isn't even wet.

2. Why does this old man have babies?

3. Why did he let the water flood the basement without moving his babies to safety?

The old man seems to be in such a panic; none of us take the time to question him. The electricity in the basement is shut off, so it's completely dark. Two of us slowly walk down the steps into the waist-deep water, and with our flashlights, we began to scan the basement. The man shouts, "They are near the north wall!"

It's a very large basement, which seems even more expansive due to the darkness.

As we move toward the north wall, a voice cries out from the dark, "Howdy, partner; what's your name?"

Another voice says, "Hey buddy, welcome to my castle."

Another voice asks, "So, how is your day?"

Now we are startled and extremely confused, because these are the strangest-sounding babies any of us have ever heard. Finally, the old man yells, "Be careful not to put your hand inside their cage, they can slice your fingers right off!"

Wait, what did he say? My flashlight scans more urgently, and finally, I see what is actually speaking to us--five very large macaws! These giant birds are his babies! Well, it takes two of us to carry each of these massive bird cages through the water and up the stairs to safety; all the while, we struggle to make sure that none of the tips of our fingers accidentally enter the cage. So now I can see why the man didn't bring his babies out of the basement himself. While I don't think the older gentleman had been honest with 911 dispatch about what his emergency was, after seeing these beautiful birds in the light, I am glad to rescue them. The man is visibly touched, and expresses to all of us his sincere gratitude. He tells us that these birds have been part of his family for over forty-years.

Truck 9 returns to service, and back to the fire station, a bit after 2000 hours (8:00 p.m.), just in time for me to pull my fire gear off the truck and switch over to Med 14, for my eight-hour, midnight shift on the ambulance. I am soaked, from top to bottom, in part because of the flooded basement, but mostly due to the torrential rain that we have just come out of. I get undressed and wring the water out my shirt, pants, underwear, and socks and place them on the radiator in the bedroom. I don't have a change of clothes, and as a fairly new guy, I don't want to tell anyone, for fear of being ripped for being unprepared. So I just sit on my bed, with a blanket wrapped around my naked body. Nearly twenty minutes pass and I start to fall asleep, when the paramedic rushes in to inform me that dispatch is calling us on the radio, to send us out on a water rescue incident.

I acknowledge that I have heard her and am on my way to the ambulance. But she stands there in the doorway looking at me to make sure that I actually get up out of bed and don't fall back to sleep. But I can't just pop up out of the bed; remember, I am completely naked. I reassure her again that

I'm up and on my way. She finally leaves, and I launch into full get-dressed-quick mode. My clothes are scorching hot but still completely soggy. I sprint over to the ambulance and take my position in the passenger's front seat. There isn't much on earth more vexing than sitting in a pair of wet, soggy underwear. When we arrive on the scene, we find a motorist who has driven under an overpass that was full of water and is now stranded, with the water rising over the hood of the vehicle. We announce to dispatch that we have arrived and have found a motorist stranded in an expanding pool of water.

I step out of the vehicle, and the cold temperature smacks me right in my face. The temperature has dropped nearly thirty-five degrees since we had rescued the Old Man's babies (birds). It was eighty degrees outside this afternoon when we started, and now it has fallen to only forty-five degrees, and I am only wearing a half-dried t-shirt and some soggy-bottom pants. The responding fire company has not arrived, and we can see that the water is starting to rise over the trapped vehicle's windows. There is a woman inside the car; she apparently tried to run her car through the water to get to the other side of the street where her subdivision entrance is. But after she drove her vehicle through the middle of the flooded viaduct, the car stalled, and she even lost electrical power to the vehicle. The loss of power prevents her from lowering the power windows. So I eventually do what I had no desire to do--I grab the window punch (a small glass- breaking device the size of a large ink pen), and I walk down into the rising water. As I walk into the chilly water, I realize immediately that the difference between this water and the water that was in the old man's basement isn't just temperature. This time I don't have any fire boots or bunker pants on!

I press through the water, and by the time I get to the vehicle, the water is right at the top of my stomach. I press the needle point of the window punch right up against the driver's side window. In less than a second, the window crumbles into a thousand little green pieces. The lady stands up in the seat and climbs out of the window onto my back. I step away from the vehicle and then attempt to let her down from off my back, but she clutches my neck tightly and begs, "Please don't let me down, I'm scared!"

I don't think she is really scared; I just think she doesn't want to get wet. I carry her through the water and back to dry ground; I figure she is at least keeping me warm. The woman is extremely grateful, and even offers to take me home with her to dry off and get a little rest. Though in my current condition that offer sounds tempting, I decline on the basis that I don't believe my new wife would approve. We are released from that scene, and I would love to tell you that was the last incident of the night. Unfortunately, over the following six hours, we conduct seven more water rescues throughout the south end of Louisville. I have never been more miserable in my life than that fateful day. There were moments that I feel as if Iam going to die from the pain of the cold, wet wind, as the temperature plunges into the low forties. It may be in part that I have been without sleep for nearly 48 hours, but quitting actually crossed my mind.

As I stand in the cold, wet elements of the night, I remember a passage out of my favorite book that reads, [15]*"Pain lasts only for a night, but relief and gladness will come in the morning."* I think, *This may be the most miserable day of my short career, but in the summation of all of my days on the*

---

[15]   (David)

department, the 24-hour good days far outweigh the few bad days. This is what people need to remember when facing the difficult days of their lives, of their marriages, or when facing the challenges of loved ones; just push through the miserable 24 hours by believing that the next 24 hours will bring a return of joy and gladness.

{LESSON 19} "Overcome the pain of today with the hopefulness of tomorrow."

Around seven-thirty in the morning, we make it back to the firehouse, pull into the bay, and my relief is standing there waiting for me. And without any fanfare, the most miserable day is finally over. Just like the passage says, "Relief came in the morning."

One Friday afternoon around 1600 hours (4:00 p.m.), Paramedic Thermis and I have just delivered a patient to the hospital emergency room and were preparing to get back to the fire station and be relieved by the second shift crew. We both clean and sanitize the ambulance, load the stretcher back into the truck, and are preparing to leave the hospital parking lot. We are less than a mile away from the fire station, where our relief crew is awaiting our arrival. So, we decide not to announce to dispatch that we are actually available to receive requests for service. Unfortunately, no sooner do we drive less than a block away than Dispatch announces an emergency incident right around the corner from our current position. Thermis picks up the radio microphone and gets ready to inform Dispatch that we are available to take this run, but I'm tired, hungry, and ready to get off this ambulance, so I try to coerce him not to call in, because we are almost back to the station.

Thermis just smiles and says, "Somebody needs our help."

Well, what can I say to that? So Thermis and I make a U-turn, switch on the lights and sirens, and go speeding to help a man who is reportedly experiencing chest pains. We pull up to the address and park in the driveway of this small apartment building. Thermis grabs the portable heart monitor, I grab the medical bag and oxygen tank, and we rush to the apartment door that's in the interior hallway of the building. I knock on the apartment door, and a voice from inside yells, "Come on in, it's not locked!"

Thermis and I walk in, and the first thing we notice is the overwhelming stench of human urine and feces. The second thing that is very noticeable, is that there isn't any furniture in the living room, and as we walk in further, we can see that there's no furniture in any of the rooms. But there is a hospital bed and a sickly-looking man lying in it. Thermis reaches the bed first (mainly because I slow up after the initial whiff at the door). Thermis greets the sickly-looking man, and introduces both of us.

Thermis then asks, "So I hear you are having chest pains?"

The man sheepishly confesses, "No, I am not having chest pains. I just need some help."

So I'm thinking, *What? You mean I could be back at the fire station, sitting at the table scarfing down the lunch that I had not had a chance to eat, but you lied, so now I'm here in this stink hole?*

Thermis asks the man if he is sick or in pain. The man replies, "I can't move. I'm a paraplegic, and I don't have anyone to help me." Thermis asks the man how this happened. The man then shares his story. "Three years ago, I was healthy and strong. I had a beautiful wife, two sons and a daughter, a gorgeous home, and a thriving business, until one day I was driving home from work and a drunk driver crashed into my vehicle. I woke up in the hospital, just glad to be alive, but I couldn't move my body. Me and my family were hopeful that the effects could be reversed, but they never changed. My wife stuck with me for a while, but she eventually left--she said she didn't sign up for this. My kids came around for a while, but I haven't seen them in nearly a year. The nurse is supposed to come once a day, but she hasn't been here since last week. The last time she was here she put some food and water next to me and left--I haven't seen her since."

Thermis interrupts the man, "So you need some food?"

The man continues, "I don't care about the food; I just want someone to clean me!"

Thermis pulls the man's covers back from off his body, and he is completely plastered with urine and feces from his chest down to his feet. Then this man looks over at me and asks, "Please clean me."

Now, you need to understand, I'm an immature 23-year-old male, and at this point in my life, I don't like washing myself. I'm nearly gagging from the dreadful urine smell. I am completely grossed out by this pale, naked man that has been colored bright yellow and dark brown from the wet and dry poo-poo glued all over his body. I'm also agitated because of the absence of the caregivers that are being paid to care for this man. Now I'm outraged at the nerve of this man, to look me in the eyes and dare ask me to go outside of my job description and do for him what his own family refused to do! I think to myself, *Clean you? There is a zero chance that I'm going to clean you!*

I turn to look and see the face of Paramedic Thermis. Surely he is as grossed out and offended as I am. As I look at his face, I can tell he is grossed out, but he opens his mouth and he says, "Sure, I will clean you."

Thermis then proceeds to go get a pan of soapy warm water, and with a washcloth, he begins to gently cleanse this man's naked body. He doesn't just wash the filth from his torso; he starts by washing the man's hair. He washes the man from head to toe, with the gentleness and care that one would give to their own loved one. Thermis' tenderness causes tears to fall from the man's eyes. As I watch this genuine display of compassion, I am embarrassed and ashamed of myself, and my heart is convicted by the pure human kindness being displayed before me. I help Thermis sanitize the man's bed and replace his sheets with some clean ones. We spend nearly two hours with the man. Thermis even takes the time to contact a few agencies and organizations that can get the man some stable assistance.

So what can happen in a day? Thermis provided more than medical care--he healed that man's emotional and mental state, he restored the man's dignity, and he taught a selfish, immature young man the powerful lessons of compassion and kindness. Over the next twenty-one years of my Louisville Fire Department career, I would always remember these compelling lessons and always tried to implement this level of grace when delivering medical care.

Thermis' selfless attitude is the perfect example of the heart and spirit of a true rescuer. Thank you, Thermis.

{LESSON 20} "True compassion is always administered with humility and has the power to bring healing to the giver as well as the receiver."

CHAPTER 14
What Can Happen In A Day

In Chapter 5 of this book, I started to share with you how my first day on the fire company went, and the long discouraging speech that my captain gave me. Now, I will share with you, the rest of the story.

After my first day, I spent the next seven months there at Engine Company Ten under the leadership of Captain Dodd. We responded together to numerous commercial and residential fires, car fires, hazardous materials incidents, motor vehicle accidents, training exercises, and countless emergency medical incidents. It felt like Captain Dodd and I were actually beginning to build a decent working relationship. The first few months that I was on the job, Captain Dodd spent the better part of each duty day berating me for my lack of firefighting knowledge. He would regularly attempt to humiliate me in front of the other station members, and while on emergency incidents he generally could find multiple ways of embarrassing me in the presence of other fire companies and even the general public. He was especially talented at asking me a question for which he knew that I had no answer and then shaming me for not knowing-- though he spent very little time actually teaching me.

I just really worked harder to try and please my captain and to raise my performance to meet his expectations. So as the months passed, his constant scolding me for my perceived lack of knowledge slowed down considerably, and I felt like I had made good progress in earning Captain Dodd's respect. Then, one evening in March, toward the end of my probationary year, it was time for Captain Dodd to complete my final evaluation and give his recommendation for my employment being retained or terminated.

Nearly an hour after dinner, I am in the kitchen preparing to make the guys some dessert, so I am gathering the ingredients for some of my "Sugar Tooth Oatmeal Raisin Cookies," when the house intercom tone sounds, and the voice behind it is that of Major Bert. He says in his Swedish but serious voice, "Firefighter Ford, report to my office immediately."

My heart is immediately startled--I mean, I have never been summoned to the major's office. What could he possibly want? His office is only twenty feet away, so I arrive quickly to his open door, and understanding protocol, I knock gently, and stand at the door until he responds or invites me inside.

"Michael, come in and sit down.," he says in a very sharp tone. "Mr. Ford, do you know why you are here?"

I shake my head in nervous bewilderment, "No, sir."

Then he spouts in frustration, "You don't know why you are here! Your captain has just recommended that your employment be terminated! And you don't know why you are here!"

My mouth drops open; I'm completely stunned. I ask, "Why?"

Major Bert interrupts, "Why? Your captain says you are lazy, you're incapable of learning the fire instruction materials, and that he has tried repeatedly to teach you, but you don't retain any of the information! So what do you have to say about this?"

For a moment, nothing comes out of my mouth; thoughts are rapidly racing through my mind. How do I answer these hurtful accusations presented against me by my own captain? You need to understand that the Louisville Fire Department operates under a paramilitary structure, and we have been methodically indoctrinated concerning the respect and reverence you are expected to yield to your superior officer.

"Mr. Ford, do you have anything to say!" comes Major Bert's last warning.

Then I burst out, "Yes, sir. My captain is a liar!"

Oh my God, when I call my captain a liar, Major Bert takes it as complete blasphemy. "Did you just call your captain a liar!"

I reply, "Yes, sir. I don't know any other way to explain it. But he is a liar! He may actually think that I don't know anything, for one main reason--he has never taken the time to teach me! But it doesn't matter, because I have learned on my own. I have gotten some of the other company members to help train me. He spends so much time trying to embarrass me with frivolous questioning that he never takes the time to find out what I know. And Major, I'm telling you that I know all of my probationary material and more! All you have to do is quiz me yourself! You check out my knowledge."

Major Bert's anger is quieted for a moment; I think he is thrown off by this new revelation and the challenge presented to him. He asks, "You want me to quiz you?"

I respond, "Yes, sir. If you quiz me, then you will know which one of us is telling the truth, and then you can decide what to do."

Major Bert reaches across his desk, picks up the probationary booklet, folds it open to the middle of the book, and begins to fire questions directly at me. At first, he asks the questions with a skeptic's cynicism, but as I answer each one with clarity and accuracy, his tone against me begins to soften. He asks me nearly twenty questions without me missing one. Major Bert pauses. He tells me, with still an ounce of skepticism, "Let's go out to the apparatus floor, and let us see how well you know that fire truck."

We make our way over to the fire truck, where Major Bert points at each closed compartment door and asks me, "What's in this one?" Without fail, I name each item, including the compartments with forty and fifty tools in them.

Now my confidence speaks up, "Major, ask me the truck serial number, ask me about the pump pressures, ask me about the specifications of each of the tools and equipment!" I am feeling extremely emotional now, and fighting tears back. "I know my captain doesn't know that I know, because he didn't teach me!"

Major Bert puts his hand on my shoulder and says softly, "I believe you, Mike. I believe you--your captain is a liar." He tells me not to worry about it, that he is going to take care of it.

Major Bert walks back into his office, and I go back to the

kitchen to put the cookie ingredients away. I'm not in the mood to bless anyone with my "Sugar Tooth Oatmeal Raisin Cookies" tonight. Moments later, the house intercom tone sounds--it's Major Bert again, but this time: "Captain Dodd, report to my office immediately!"

I watch Captain Dodd stroll past the kitchen and into Major Bert's office. The next thing I hear is lots of screaming and hollering, mostly coming from Major Bert, which is very strange, coming from a man that I have never previously heard raise his voice. I can't make out what is being said, plus I am still too nervous about how this was going to affect my own fate. Finally, Captain Dodd comes storming out of the office, bypassing the kitchen where I am standing.

Major Bert comes out of his office next, and cracks open the see-through kitchen door, and says to me, "Michael, I'm going to get you a real captain in here."

I don't really know what he means by that statement, but by the time I arrive to my next on-duty day, Captain Dodd has been transferred to another fire company out in the east end of town. I am retained in my position by the fire department and approved to pass my probationary period.

After my first and second year on the department ends, I realize that my firefighter career isn't exactly traveling in the right direction. I am twenty-two years old, and giving very little attention to setting any goals, or growing into a greater understanding of my profession. As far as I am concerned, I was enjoying the camaraderie of the firehouse; the excitement of firefighting; the thrill of speeding through the streets, lights and sirens, on "Big RED," the fire truck; the prestige of donning the badge, the uniform, and the fire turnout gear. And at age twenty-two, I think that I am nearly rich, because the fire department is paying me a salary of nearly $28,000. And I am extremely content and satisfied with the status quo.

In my third year, I am reassigned from Engine 10 to Quint Company 9 and Med Unit 14. At first, it's tough getting used to the slower pace and the grumpy old men that are still part of this fire company. But over the next year, the older crew eventually retire, so the department ships in a group of young guys to fill their positions: Firefighter Heathcliff, Firefighter Andy, and Firefighter Billy, along with Senior Firefighter Jon, and Sergeant Man is also transferred over from my old fire station, Truck 8/Engine 10. Over the next three years at Quint 9, this would be the most fun, enjoyable, entertaining time and crew that I will ever have on the fire department. When I first arrive, no one ever wants to so much as visit this station, let alone suffer being assigned to Quint 9, but over the next three years, our station will become known as the "Fun House."

Anytime you bring a new team together there is that awkward period of getting to know each other's strengths, weaknesses, personalities, likes and dislikes. It is a time when everyone struggles to find their niche within the structure of the team. But for some strange reason, this crew of distinctive personalities seems to easily fit together like a first grader's puzzle. The captain is a large, serious-faced older man, but Captain Danny seems to have a real playful streak, which is the perfect temperament for leading and protecting the birthing of the new "Fun House." At first the new crew starts playing some games of basketball in the evening. Then we add some football games in the afternoon. Then one of us brings in a Play Station video game, and we start playing Madden football tournaments, then Tiger Woods golf tournaments, then NASCAR racing, then Call of Duty; we declare full all-out toilet paper roll wars--you get the picture (toilet paper war – fire department toilet paper rolls were delivered to the fire stations in boxes of 300 roll packages. Two or three of these boxes would be brought into the bedroom and thrown across the room with a ferocious velocity at the opposing firefighters. Note: No toilet paper was hurt or wasted in these fights). Next, someone in the crew talks us all into going paintballing after work, and eventually we all buy our own paintball guns and gear packs and start meeting weekly on Sergeant Man's land around his house for all-out paintball wars. Back at the fire station we start watching movies together late into the night--we are just flat-out enjoying each other's company. We are quickly passing through the coworkers and friends stages and are rapidly becoming a company of brothers.

At the end of our first year together, around Christmas time, Firefighter Heathcliff comes into the firehouse looking like a baby Santa, bearing a colossal bag of gifts for the entire crew. Now it isn't unusual for fire crews to give each other gifts at Christmas--normally the gift is a new flashlight, screwdriver, coffee mug, or something of that practical nature that a firefighter can use at work. Heathcliff hands all of us these large, weird-shaped packages. We are all excited to open them, so we do so together.

"Oh my God!" "These are crazy!" is our response after cracking open the gift wrapping and seeing our new fire station toys! Heathcliff has bought each of us a new Laser Tag gun, pack, and accessories. These gifts will rocket our firehouse to official "coolest" firehouse status. We can't wait for nightfall to descend, so that the festivities can begin. We choose teams, then turn out all of the lights in the fire station, and the only thing that you can see is the infrared beams of light pointing from the guns, and the glowing red lights, pulsating on the chests, shoulders, and backs of the packs that each of us were wearing. We are grown men, acting and playing with the excitement and exuberance of children. Not only the first night, but many subsequent nights, we play for hours, hiding under beds, around corners, on the rooftops, chasing and shooting infrared light beams at each other, stopping only because of actual firefighting work or incidents that we are dispatched to.

It gets to a point where even when we are off duty we spend days together. Sometimes we travel out to the countryside on the outskirts of Louisville where Firefighter Andy and his wife Wynita had built their home on family land, and we go fishing and skeet shooting. Andy, Wynita, and I are becoming pretty good friends, but out of all the times that we had traveled out to the country for recreation, we have never made it over to Andy's house, because the fishing pond and the skeet shooting range are on his father's land. But one particular day, we need to stop by Andy's house to get the fishing poles. Firefighter Andy has a nice country home, and as I walk through the living room back to the bathroom, I notice the pictures of Andy's beautiful family. But something is very bizarre about the carved wooden name that is pasted all over each wall. The name Melissa. I think, *Who is this Melissa? Wait a minute!*

I walk back into the living room were Andy is preparing to load the truck and I holler at him, "Hey! Who is Melissa!"

Firefighter Andy's face turns beet red, and he is so surprised by the question that he just bursts with laughter, and he shouts, "Nooo! I forgot about the pictures in the hallway!"

Now I rush over to him to try and wrestle the truth out of

him, "Your wife's name isn't Wynita! I have been calling her Wynita for over five years! And she has answered to Wynita every time I called her that! She's in on this too!"

Andy can't get a single word out of his mouth, because he can't stop laughing. Even as fat tear droplets pour from his eyes. I continue, "Wait, is the whole fire company in on this-- they all know that her name isn't Wynita?" I immediately dial up Andy's wife at work, and she answers, "Hello, Michael."

I interrupt, "Don't hello me! Melissa!"

She goes silent for a moment and then goes into a full scream of embarrassing laughter. "Nooo! How did you find out?"

I tell her how ashamed I am of her. "I mean, I expect this from some silly firemen, but not from you--I expected more of you, Wynita--I mean, Melissa, or whoever you are!"

She just continues in hysterical laughter. What can happen in a day? You may find out that your friends have been playing a joke on you for the past five years! I don't think they were ever going to tell me.

Anyway, I was telling you how much fun the Quint 9 crew was having together. I have worked at jobs that were so boring, repetitive, and purposeless that I dreaded going in each day. Serving on the Louisville Fire Department was different; it felt fruitful, purposeful, and anything but boring. Moreover, working with this Quint 9 crew is a downright daily adventure. One morning I am getting dressed at home, preparing to come into work for my 24-hour duty day. When I look up, I notice that my wife is glaring at me with envious eyes, shaking her head. I am like, "What?"

She says, "Look at you! Look at how giddy you are about going to work!"

Then she says something profound that I have never forgotten, "You get to go to work!"

I try to deny it. "I don't get to go to work, I have to go to work. It's my job."

But I can't even say it with a straight face. She is right--this job, this career that I have is such a privilege! It's not like any other job that I have ever had. Most people have jobs that they loathe. I mean, here I am, six o'clock in the morning, with a big fat clown smile on my face, unknowing, but excited about what adventure today's 24-hour shift will present to me. So my wife is correct--I do "get to" go to work.

That afternoon, after lunch, as the Quint 9 crew is finishing cleanup, the district chief stops by the fire station and brings a memorandum from the chief of the department, informing us that the sergeant's promotional test will be administered in October. That gives us four months to buckle down and study for the test. Once the district chief exits the room, the guys and I begin to discuss who among us might take this promotional test. After much discussion and debate, it is agreed that we all will take this upcoming promotional exam. So we set our sights on promotion. We make plans to commit ourselves to studying together at the firehouse, for three hours daily, over the next three months. The plan is that we will start today, but Firefighter Bill reminds us that we are right in the middle of a Madden (video game) football tournament, and that we need to at least finish that. We all agree that we need to finish the video game tournament, but starting next day, we will get right to our studies.

Our next duty day, true to our word, as soon as we finish eating lunch, we all gather in the TV room, carrying our study materials. It is fun to see us all buckle down together, to push toward our goal of promotion. We sit on chairs and couches for ten minutes, exchanging questions and answers, until Firefighter Andy asks Firefighter Heathcliff a question that he can't answer. Andy makes a comment about how he is going to score higher than Heathcliff on the promotional test. Heathcliff quips back at him, "You said that you were going to outscore me in that Madden championship last on day, but I whipped that butt!"

And that is all it takes! The study session abruptly ends, and the next video game tournament begins. This is generally the story of the next four months--we continue in our mindset of fun and adventure. Oh, there are days that we may have gotten a little further than ten minutes, but for the most part we are never really able to muster the focus to implement quality test preparation. We really do have a goal to reach promotion, but we never allow our goal to dictate our actions.

{LESSON 21} "To reach success, you must allow your goals to dictate your behaviors and actions!"

When October comes, all of the Quint 9 fun crew sit for the promotional exam, but none of us do well. When the results are posted and everyone is ranked according to their score, I am ranked number 35 out of about 65 firefighters that took the exam. This promotional list wouldn't expire for two years. Over the next two years, the department promotes thirty firefighters to the position of sergeant, and then the list expires. They promote thirty--that means I was only five spots away from promotion, but I missed out! Then I am really disgusted with myself. I think, *What if I had actually prepared, actually studied, actually applied some serious actions to my goal. I would have certainly reached my goal of promotion.*

{LESSON 22} "Never allow people or laziness to distract you from purposeful action and the pursuit and achievement of your goals and dreams."

I determine in my mind that this will be the last time I give a poor, insufficient effort in the pursuit of my goals and dreams.

A few weeks later, the battalion chief stops by our station and calls me into the captain's office. He informs me that I have completed my sixth year on the department and no longer have to be assigned to ride the Med Unit (ambulance). This means that I am now a tenured firefighter and can spend my whole day assigned to the fire company (fire truck). "Yes!" I exclaim with great excitement. The battalion chief says that there is only one catch. I will have to leave Quint Company 9. "No!" I complain, "I love this fire station and its crew. I don't want to leave."

The battalion chief explains, "You can either write a letter stating that you don't want to be removed from being assigned to the Med Unit, or you will be reassigned to another fire company. You have until next on-day to decide."

After the battalion chief leaves, I go and inform the "Fun Crew" of my dilemma. They of course immediately try to persuade me, coerce me to stay by reminding me of all the fun times that we have experienced together and all the upcoming festivities that I will miss if I leave. That evening as I lie on my bed contemplating what should be my next step, I think about how comfortable and happy I am in my current position. I think about how I am so comfortable with my current state that I could stay here for the next fourteen years and finish my career here. Then I remember my goal of being promoted. This goal of being promoted isn't just about me. I want promotion so that as I am pushing my daughter and four sons to work hard, dream big, and reach high, I won't be the hypocrite dad that tells his kids not to smoke even as he's blowing cigarette smoke from his mouth and nostrils. I want to be an affirmative example of how every goal is attainable with the persistent, tenacious pursuit.

As I am now leaning toward leaving Quint 9, but not quite fully persuaded, I have a flashback to the first time I considered going after the sergeant's promotion. I was in my third year on the department, at Engine Company 10. I am not sure how my sergeant received the news of my plan to sit for the exam, but somehow he was informed. Sergeant Tarry approached me on the apparatus floor, near the overhead doors, and came up to me, placed his right arm around my shoulders, as if to indicate warm friendship, and to help me more easily swallow the poison that he was about to inject into my mind. He said, "Ford, I heard that you're thinking about taking the Sergeant's promotional exam?"

I nodded my head in affirmation, believing that he was about to share with me some good tips on some of the questions that I might find on the test, or maybe some quality test-taking strategies. He continued, "Ford, I don't know if you are ready to take this test, because this test is hard, and you aren't very smart. You are probably going to end up embarrassing yourself and embarrassing your fire company. I think what you should do is just concentrate on being a firefighter and be satisfied that you have a job."

I kept a straight face and nodded my head in confirmation that I understood what he was saying. But truth be told, I was crushed! Someone that I respected, in his position, should have encouraged me, built me up, but instead, he spoke words to destroy me. As I lie on my bed at Quint 9 remembering this incident, I think, *Who is he? Who is he to appraise my intellect or to determine how far I should or could reach? Who does he think he is, to prognosticate my future?* Then I remembered lesson #2 that I had learned at the Academy, "***Use your adversary's negativity to fuel your fire to succeed!***"

And with that, my mind is made up. I will leave the "Fun House" to go in hot pursuit of my career goals.

Three days later I am informed that I will be reassigned to Truck Company 4, located in one of the busiest fire sections of the city. When I hear this, I am a bit nervous. Truck Company 4 is widely known as the premier fire company in the Louisville Fire Department, and considered by most to be the flagship Truck Company of the department. I am even more apprehensive once I hear who will be my commanding officer: Captain D. Wayne, a no-nonsense, cuss-you-out, aggressive firefighting machine, is what I had heard about him. Upon my first day of arrival at Truck Company 4, Captain D. Wayne calls me into his office. After I sit down, he begins the conversation by clearly spelling out the company rules, and his expectations for me as a new Truck 4 member.

Then he asks me, "Tell me, in what firefighting skill areas are you deficient?"

I pause for a moment to consider how I should answer his inquiry. Not that I don't know the answer, but because the most truthful answer is that I am deficient in numerous areas! How do I now explain to my new captain that I am most deficient in the areas of small tools, power saws, ground ladders, aerials, breaching, roof operations, ropes, ventilation, and vehicle rescue tools and operations? How do I tell the company commander of the department's flagship truck that his newest member is deficient in his occupational skillset because he has been having a good time at the "Fun House?" I think about not telling him about my deficiencies, but I would hate for him to see my deficiencies for himself during an emergency incident where lives are at stake. I think about blaming my former captains, explaining that they failed to train me and they are to blame for my shortcomings, but that isn't the truth.

I decide to come clean with the truth. I expose all of my deficiencies and explain to Captain Wayne that I am deficient because I have been extremely lazy in my training and studies over the past three years. I tell him that I am really ashamed of myself for my lack of maturity and have decided to make a positive change in my work habits. I also inform him of my goal and desire to earn promotion to sergeant. I am expecting Captain Wayne to give me one of his infamous "cussings," but he does not. He just says, "Okay, your training starts now."

Captain Wayne immediately gets on the station intercom and calls for the entire crew to meet him at the fire truck. For the next four hours the Truck 4 crew rides the streets of beautiful West Louisville, and stop at a house on seemingly every corner. Captain D. Wayne has us pull up to a house and simulate as if it was a structure on fire. He has me go to the rear of the truck and determine what size ladder is required, and then I deploy the ladder to get to the roof. After four hours of deploying an eight-foot, sixteen-foot, twenty-two-foot, and a thirty-five-foot ladder, I declare that I was no longer deficient in that area. This is how Captain D. Wayne worked with me on all my deficient firefighting skills. One day we spent hours training on power saws, one day small tools, one day aerials, one day breaching, one day roof operations, one day ropes, one day ventilation, and another day vehicle rescue tools and operations. Out of all the stories that I had heard concerning Captain D. Wayne, no one ever spoke of the fact that he was a master trainer. I spend the next two years not only being trained by Captain Wayne, but our crew also fight quite a number of significant structure fires, where I grow in knowledge and experience.

Near the end of my second year at "Mighty Truck Company 4," the battalion chief comes in and handed the firefighters a memo describing the date and time of the upcoming sergeant's promotional exam. Some of the guys deliberate with each other whether they will sit for the exam. I just calmly walk out of the room; there won't be any need of deliberation for me. My mind has been fixated and my heart set on this goal since the last missed promotional opportunity. I determine that this time will be different; I read the five-hundred-page Standard Operating Procedures book and the one-hundred page LFD Rules book, highlighting every superficially important point that each book describes. Then I read through both books again; this time I voice-record myself reading every highlighted point in the books. Finally, I listen to these voice-recorded audios every day, for at least four hours each day, for the subsequent three months leading up to the promotional exam. I listen to these audio files of myself quoting lines from the LFD reference books every time I step into my car.

My kids hate this; they say, "No Daddy, not again! Please play some music."

I tell them, "There won't be any music playing in the car for a while. Daddy is studying for his test. Don't you want Daddy to do good?"

They reply with reluctance in their voices, "Yes, sir." Poor babies; truth be told, they hear so many hours of those audios, I think they all could sit for the exam and pass.

When test day comes, we all walk into a very large room; there are nearly a hundred firefighters there seeking promotion. I am nervous but silently confident. We sit down in our seats and are presented with the one hundred and ten question exam and one hour to complete it. Over the next forty-five minutes, as I maneuver through the test all the way to the last page of questions, I think, *I don't think I've answered a single question incorrectly.* When it is all finished, I have scored 107 correct out of the 110 questions given, and I am ranked 13th out of the 97 firefighters that sat for the exam. A few months later, during the promotional ceremony, I am called to the stage to receive my sergeant's rank insignia. My wife and five children (the youngest was still in the womb) escort me to the stage, take pictures with the chief and the mayor, and even pin the sergeant's chevrons on my collar. What a grand day! For my wife, children, mom, dad, brothers, and sisters to be there to share in my moment of success--and why not? They are a huge part of what fueled me. There are others in the audience that made the celebration even more sweet. Specifically, two others that I would love to appreciate for helping to energize me to promotion--two of my adversaries, Sgt. Spade and Sgt. Tarry, both are in attendance that day. I learn a valuable lesson that day.

{LESSON 23} "The opposition and obstructions that you overcome in your life are the very ingredients that give your victory its sweet flavor."

In my third year as a sergeant, I am transferred to Engine Company 7, which at the time is the oldest active fire station in the country. I really don't want to be reassigned to this station, because I have gotten comfortable with my previous fire company, Engine 21. I am forced to leave a good department friend, Firefighter Damon, and have to learn a new crew. This new crew is already a pretty tight-knit group, so I constantly feel like an outsider. There is Firefighter William, who is brash and pushy and constantly picks fights with me; we eventually become great friends. Then there is Firefighter Luke (The Portland Puncher), an antagonistic, controversial, combative, sarcastic trouble-maker, and I enjoy working with him from the very first day. Finally, there is my company commander, Captain Dez. I eventually come to really appreciate this crew, especially after we start to mingle in some of the entertaining activities that I have brought with me from my days at the "Fun House," though I am still committed to achieving my goals.

One day, I share with Captain Dez that I want to prepare myself for the promotion to captain, and I ask him if he will begin to show me how to manage the employee payroll, sick and vacation leave, scheduling, incident reports, daily log and any other LFD forms. Over the next few months, Captain Dez shows me all of it. I start spending each day completing each of these tasks, until the day that I feel comfortable with each one. One day I come in to work a bit tired; it is my day to cook, and I still need to get my apparatus daily work accomplished.

At the end of the evening, after I have completed all my assignments, cooked two fantastic meals, and completed all of my incident reports, Captain Dez tells me that I needed to make sure I finish all of the company reports. I'm thinking, *Company reports? He means, all of his reports!*

I am really not happy, but I just say, "Yes, sir, I will take care of them."

I walk out of the kitchen and into the captain's office, and as I sit down to work on the incident reports, I realize that they aren't the only reports Captain Dez hasn't completed. The daily log, payroll, time book, scheduling, and the school report also have not been completed. I really feel frustrated by the thought that Captain Dez is taking advantage of me and my goodwill. While I am fuming to myself, a very wise thought infiltrates my psyche. I remembered the classic movie, [16]*The Karate Kid.* How young Daniel Larusso has the goal of learning karate, so he employs the help of the martial arts master Mr. Miyagi. Daniel's first karate practice days were filled with seemingly insignificant chores of washing and applying wax to a bunch of old vintage vehicles, painting a fence, and sanding a deck. Daniel eventually gets fed up with these seemingly meaningless chores, because he has not understood that each action he completes is actually instilling an essential karate skill. So, my completing each company commander report or task was just me "waxing on and waxing off" in order to reach my goal! Do you realize how many people have missed out on growth opportunities because they felt as if it was beneath them or it wasn't in their job description? I almost ruin a really fantastic opportunity due to my immaturity. Well, I complete all of the incomplete LFD assignments for that night and

---

16   (Weintraub, 1984)

every night for the next year. I have a renewed determination to reach my promotional goal.

In 2006, I begin my test preparation for the company commander's exam. This is unlike the sergeant's exam that I took a few years back. This exam is a three-day assessment that evaluates the candidates' written and oral communication skills, their proficiency in handling personnel issues, their ability to manage a fire emergency incident, and their understanding and application of the LFD rules and standard operating procedures.

I again read the five-hundred-page Standard Operating Procedures book and the one-hundred page LFD Rules book, highlighting every superficially important point that applies to the company commander's position. Then I read through both books again; this time I voice- record myself reading every highlighted point in the books. Finally, I listen to these voice- recorded audios every day, for at least four hours each day, for the subsequent months leading up to the promotional exam. I listen to these audio files of myself quoting lines from the LFD reference books every time I step into the car, or while I sit by the pool on my vacation, and any other time that I have a free moment.

The first day of the exam, all the candidates are placed in a small waiting room where most of us have to stand because there aren't enough chairs. There are nearly sixty candidates in the room; everyone mostly is just in casual conversation. I am standing up against the south wall, thinking through a few mental notes. One of the more boisterous personalities in the room inadvertently attracts everyone's attention when he begins to suggest which of us in the room will rank in the top

20 on this exam. He calls out the names of a number of guys in the room, including himself, that will make up the top 20. When he fails to mention my name, I think:

1. He is a complete idiot for opening his mouth in the first place.

2. His prognostication is obviously false, because it doesn't include me.

3. {LESSON 23} ***"The opposition and obstructions that you overcome in your life are the ingredients that give victory its sweet flavor."*** His big mouth and his underestimation of me are going to make my success even more enjoyable!

You see, most people make snap judgments about who you are, your intellect, your talent, and your worth. Because of this, they miss out on the quality and the value that you could add to their lives. People don't know the work and effort that you have put in behind closed doors.

Eventually, we are all called in to a large open room filled with lots of tables and chairs, and we are seated for the first day of the exam. The proctors present the candidates with a multi-layered personnel issue, requiring us to take thirty minutes and utilize our written communication skills and our understanding of LFD Rules and Regulations to systematically work through each issue to properly handle the emergency situation. Once we are finished, we are then taken into a private room and given ten minutes to record our oral explanation of how we would handle this layered personnel issue. Once I enter the private room to give my oral presentation, the proctor informs me that I have ten minutes and that the time will start when I signal that I'm ready. I give the proctor the signal that I am ready, and I begin my verbal presentation. After a few minutes of talking, I signal to the proctor that I am finished. The proctor looks back at me and gives me a very puzzled expression, and motions to me to continue, because I have taken only four minutes. But I can't continue; I have said everything that I think should be done and said to properly handle this personnel issue. So the proctor turns off the recording, and shakes her head a bit, and says, "All the other candidates took at least eight minutes."

When I leave the building, I started really beating myself up about my perceived mistakes in taking today's portion of the test. I leave the building so discouraged that for a few moments I consider not returning for the next day's portion of the exam. However, I quickly expel those thoughts from my mind because I understand:

{LESSON 24} "You don't stand a chance of success, if you don't bother to show up," and {LESSON 25} "You beat most of the competition, just by showing up!"

When I arrive at the test site the next morning, I am informed that seven candidates didn't show up for this next phase—well, I beat them already. I finish the last two test phases and am eventually informed that I have ranked number 13 out of 61 candidates that sat for the exam. When I review the results and the comments that the test assessors had written, I find out that I scored the highest on the personnel problem. The assessors comment, "Very detailed, succinct, well-organized thoughts. Thanks for not filibustering the time!" Wow, I was worried for nothing. A few months later, I am promoted to captain. The guys at Engine Company 7 invite my mother and father, my wife and five children over to the firehouse to have some cake and ice cream to help celebrate my promotion. My dad is especially proud; he is even allowed to pin the captain's rank insignia on my collar.

I am immensely excited and nervous when I arrive to my first assignment as company commander. I am assigned as the pool officer in Battalion 2. This just means that I'm not assigned to my own fire company, but I will be sent temporarily to fire stations where the company officer is absent due to vacation, injury or sickness. Most of the LFD captains despise the thought of being assigned to the pool, because they view it as being beneath being assigned your own company, and they believe it is a punishment or a sign of some disrespect. It can also be a hassle, due to the fact that you are constantly having to pack all your gear from fire station to fire station, and it feels a bit like an unstable life. But for me, I just look at the situation from a different angle. When I was hired on the department, I was just satisfied to have been selected from the two thousand applicants that had applied; and after such a rocky start, from Sgt. Slade promising to fire me in the academy, to my first captain trying to fire me in my first year, to Sgt. Tarry insisting that I wasn't smart enough to be a sergeant, I am just so very proud to have arrived at this day, where I have been promoted considerably farther than where any of my haters had predicted for my career.

One individual asked me if I was upset that the chief's staff placed me in the substitute captain's pool. See, this is a serious problem with many people; they filter their thoughts through these negative assumptions that somebody is doing them wrong, that there is some huge conspiracy against them.

In some cases, this may be true, but if we focus in on the negative possibilities, we may miss out on the hidden opportunities in these kairos moments. When I was playing football at Louisville Male High School, I won the starting varsity fullback position in my junior year, but the coaches also instructed me to get suited up for the Junior Varsity team games. In my young teenaged mind, I really felt disrespected and showed my displeasure through my negative posture, words, and attitude.

The head varsity coach pulled me to the sideline and asked me, "Boy what is your problem?!"

I shrugged my shoulders in a very pouty gesture and asked, "Why are you making me play in this stupid Junior Varsity game when I am now a Varsity starter?"

The coach smacks me on the head and explains, "You are the starting fullback on Varsity that never carries the ball, we were trying to get you some experience of carrying the ball in these JV games so that we can use you to run the ball in the Varsity games!"

Wow, because I felt disrespected, I couldn't see the opportunity that was right in my face. This was why I refused to look negatively at being a pool captain. I only viewed it as an opportunity to grow and learn.

{LESSON 26} "If we focus in on the negative possibilities, we may miss out on the hidden opportunities that life is presenting us."

After all, I was able to work at every fire station in the department. When I would work at a double house (two fire companies in the same station) I was afforded the opportunity to work with some of the best, most experienced captains, and I would glean from their knowledge and expertise regarding leading a crew, and fire suppression tactics. Sometimes I would arrive at a particular fire station due to the captain being on vacation, and I would see the companies that were not being run well, and I would learn what not to do.

They call the pool captain a substitute teacher; well, I was that substitute teacher that made sure the class did everything that the day's lesson plan called for, and I wasn't the one that you were going to get over on.

One of my first days as pool captain at Engine 16, an old veteran, Firefighter Tony, walks into my office around 11:30 p.m. and says, "Captain Ford, I am getting ready to take the service truck over to Firefighter Jack's house. His wife just called and said Jack is drunk and she needs help getting him in bed."

I pause for a moment to think this through. Firefighter Tony knows that I am a brand-new captain, and he's testing me to see what he can get away with. I tell him, "No. I'm not letting you take the service truck to go out of the station at 11:30 p.m., to travel to another firefighter's house, at the request of his wife! That has disaster written all over it."

Firefighter Tony raises his voice. "Damn, Captain! If Captain Williams was here, he would let me go!"

To which I reply very calmly but firmly, "Captain Williams isn't here today--I am. And I am telling you that you can't go."

With that, Firefighter Tony starts laughing and as he walks

away, saying, "That's okay, Captain Ford--I just wanted to see if you would let me go."

See, that was a growing experience that I wouldn't have had if not for being assigned to the pool. As a pool captain, there were daily growth experiences that helped to shape the kind of leader I would become. Instead of learning how to deal with four members who would be assigned to my company, the pool brought me in contact with hundreds of firefighters and sergeants, which allowed me to experience managing many personalities and situations. It also allowed me to be managed by an eclectic group of battalion chiefs, who taught me diverse ways of effective positive leading and diverse ways of ineffective, negative leading. I gleaned knowledge from both the good ones and the bad.

So, I remain a pool officer for two years. One Friday morning, I am detailed for 24 hours over to Quint Company 9; that's right, back to the "Fun House." It has been nearly eight years since I had left Quint Company 9, so it is a blast seeing the guys. We all spend a good hour at the kitchen table just laughing and catching up with one another. We finally disperse to go and accomplish our morning duties. When I arrived at the captain's office and review the log books, time books, and monthly duty schedule, I notice that the assigned captain has been off injured for nearly three months and that the captains detailed in to cover his absence have not completed school reports, inspection obligations, target hazard plans, street and water exams, hose changes, nor end of month reports. I realize that I will be assigned to the station for the next three duty days, so I decide to try and complete as much of the incomplete work as I can, while I am here.

So the first day, before lunch, we complete the inventory and inspection of all the tools and equipment carried on three apparatus, and complete the end of the month reports that should have been completed two weeks prior. After lunch, we complete hose changes on the Quint and the auxiliary engine; this takes nearly two hours. Next, I tell the guys to go and put on their uniform shirts so that we can go accomplish some door-to-door house inspections for a couple of hours while the weather is unseasonably warm. Well, Firefighter Jon, our twenty-year senior member, has seen quite enough. Jon looks at me with his eyes bulging out of his head, and points to the kitchen, basically demanding me to step into his office (actually it is more like his bedroom; Jon is a "coucher").

Now I have known Firefighter Jon for over ten years, and I know the level of disrespect of authority that he is capable of. Firefighter Jon's reputation in this area is very well documented. He is very well liked, but even the battalion chiefs are careful not to set him off. I once saw Major K. Lynn walk up to the service truck passenger window and order Jon to get out of the front seat so that he could ride up front. Now the normal firefighter would have just said, "Yes, sir," and would immediately comply, but not Jon. Jon replied to the battalion chief, "I'm Rosa Parks--you go to the back of the bus!" Then Jon rolled his window up.

The battalion tapped on the window and said in a very authoritative voice, "Jon, open this door and get in the back!"

Jon just smiled, and with his thumb he motioned Major Lynn to the back of the service truck saying repeatedly, "Back of the bus, back of the bus!" And you know what, the major went and sat in the back of the bus.

So, as I walk into the kitchen, I realize Jon is probably going to cuss me out. Jon says to me, "Mike, what the f--- are you doing?" I explain to him that we are just trying to get some things accomplished that need to get completed. Jon interrupts, "Damn Mike, you have f---ing changed! You have let that captain's stuff go to your head!"

Now I interrupt in frustration, "Jon, the last time we worked together I was a firefighter also, so of course you remember me in a place in my career where having fun at the fire station was a high priority, but I have been away from the Fun House for eight years. In those eight years I have grown in my maturity, work ethic, and understanding of my responsibilities. I have moved from the responsibilities of a firefighter to the responsibilities of a captain, so of course I have changed. I am better than who I used to be!"

> **{LESSON 27} "Be careful not to allow anyone or anything to keep you boxed up into who you used to be, and what you used to do, or where you came from, or your past failures and shortcomings. Declare to them with your words and actions: I have CHANGED! I am BETTER than who I used to be!"**

Surprisingly, that is good enough for Firefighter Jon, and he acquiesces to everything that I asked of him. We remain friends to this day.

One day, near the end of my second year as a captain without my own fire station, I am volunteering at a fire prevention event called "The Great Louisville Fire Drill." I am helping to clean up the debris left over from the event, when the chief of the department walks over to me and asks how I am doing. I have never really spoken to the chief before, and I don't have my name plate on, so I am a bit surprised that he knows my name. I smile and tell him that I am doing well. He tells me that he has been hearing really good things about me, and he jokes that after he read my promotional interview positon paper, he realized that maybe he should have me write some of his speeches.

I laugh, and then I ask him, "Chief, if I am doing things well, and I'm building a good reputation as a captain, and according to my evaluations, exceeding the standards, then why haven't I been given my own fire company? Have I done something wrong that I'm just not aware of."

The chief thinks for a moment, and says, "Mike, you haven't done anything wrong; sometimes it's just a matter of the squeaky wheels getting all the oil. But don't worry, I'm going to take care of it, and I think you will be very happy."

I don't exactly know what he means, but I thank him, and he walks away. The next week, a reassignment memorandum comes out from the chief's staff, and listed right near the top, is my name and me being reassigned from the captain's pool to my own fire station, Engine Company 18. Yes, I am overjoyed! Engine Company 18 is a very busy company, with plenty of structure fires, some high-rise buildings, lots of interstate and medical incidents, and it is right next to the campus of the University of Louisville. My company will be able to attend the basketball, football, track, baseball, soccer, and volleyball games. The next week when I arrive, I meet my new crew:

1. Sergeant Chad – Came into the department with me, and out of that last great Recruit Class #170

2. Firefighter Murph – "The Character"

3. Firefighter Doug – "The Farmer" or "The Old Man"

4. Firefighter Patrick – "The New Boy"

These guys help make Engine Company 18 a really great fire company. We train together, we play together, we respond to thousands of medical and fire incidents over the next three years, and we even attempt to get in good physical shape together. Convincing the crew to try and get in shape is a true chore. I've explained to you how firefighters eat each day; we really take our meals seriously. Well, in the last few years the fire service has been pounding into its members that the number one killer of firefighters is a heart attack. Consequently, many fire stations are starting to cook in a healthier way, and most are employing some exercise regimen into their daily routines. It takes some time, but eventually everyone gets on board, including "Old Man" Doug. The only issue is Firefighter Murph—he agrees to go with us, but his mouth is still complaining, and his heart is definitely not in it.

One morning, we go to the University of Louisville track stadium to get some exercise. We all leisurely walk the first four laps around the track and are scheduled to jog the next two. Well, Murph has been complaining about how he really doesn't want to do any jogging, so I figure I am really going to hear his mouth as we start the first jogging lap. And sure enough, we haven't taken three jogging steps when Firefighter Murph pulls up with a scream of pain and falls to the ground holding the back of his leg as if he is severely injured. I look back and I don't even bother to stop. This is just some more Murph antics because he doesn't want to run.

After I complete my lap, I come over to where Murph is sitting, and he is still lying on the ground. I say, "Okay, Murph, you have proven your point--you don't have to jog."

He says to me, "No, Captain, I'm not joking; I am really hurt."

He was actually hurt, and I feel bad that I left him there on the track, but because we are firefighters, we of course turn his pain into a really good laugh. We get him back to the fire station, write up an injury report, and send him home--but Murph stays until after lunch, because he loves to eat.

Later that afternoon, two of the department's Assistant Chiefs stop by the station, which is generally unusual. The crew and I stand at attention and greet them as they enter the kitchen area where we are seated. They seem to have something serious on their minds, when they state, "Captain Ford, let's go up to your office."

Now, I am a bit worried about what I've done wrong. We small talk on our way up the steps, but as we enter the office, Colonel Jeff speaks up, and asks me if I like being at Company 18.

I respond emphatically, "Yes, I love it here."

He then explains, "There is a company commander's opening on Truck Company 4 and we think that you would be the ideal captain to fill it. We think you have proven yourself to be an outstanding fire company commander, and this will be just the next step in building your experience for the next level of leadership."

Well, I am stunned, and initially suspicious of the

motivations behind this unexpected visit. I mean, are they just trying to take Engine 18 from me? Aren't there some other great captains in that district who would love to lead that company? But my maturity kicks in, and I realize that these men are here out of respect for the captain that I have become, and their offer is a testimony to how far I have grown from the young man who was almost fired in my first year to now being offered the opportunity to lead "Mighty Truck Company 4," widely known to be the premier fire company in the Louisville Fire Department, and considered by most to be the flagship Truck Company of the department. (I'm repeating this statement to poke fun at all of the former members of Truck Company 1, who believe that they are the flagship company of the department.) Though I am saddened that I will have to leave my Engine 18 crew, I agree to accept the opportunity for a new chapter and additional growth.

I work the next two years as a company commander. My crews and I serve with distinction, receiving some performance awards, and excellent performance ratings. I have gained some really good experience as a company commander and begin to believe that I am ready to take the next steps toward promotion to battalion chief. So, you already know what I do; I read the five-hundred-page Standard Operating Procedures book and the one-hundred-page LFD Rules book, highlighting every superficially important point that each book describes. Then I read through both books again; this time I voice-record myself reading every highlighted point in the books. Finally, I listen to these voice-recorded audios every day, for at least four hours each day, for the subsequent three months leading up to the promotional exam. I listen to these audio files of myself quoting lines from the LFD reference books every time I step into the car. I also sit with a few battalion chiefs and have them explain overtime hiring procedures, the daily personnel scheduling, and how to operate when you are the battalion over the command district.

This exam will be similar to the company commander's test, in that it will be broken up into three days of testing. When I arrive, I am anxious, but confident that just like I conquered the sergeant's exam and the captain's exam, I will do the same to this battalion chief's exam. Unfortunately, after three days of testing I am really upset with myself, because I feel as though I haven't performed up to my capabilities. I mean, I can live with not obtaining the promotion because I did my best, and my best wasn't good enough; but I'm having a hard time coping with the fact that I'm just underperforming. When the scores and rankings are posted, I find myself ranked number 13th again, only this time, there will be nothing to celebrate. There will only be six promotions from this two-year battalion chief's list, and I won't be one of them. For the next few days, I am really disappointed and frustrated with myself for not achieving this set goal. I spend some time in prayer and come out with some peace, knowing that though I didn't win this day, another day of opportunity will soon come. So I re-engage back to the business of leading my fire company with a positive, optimistic outlook.

The next month, as I am sitting in the captain's office, I notice that the chief has just emailed out a memorandum informing the department that there is an assistant chief's position vacant on his staff. The report instructs all interested majors/battalion chiefs to forward their resume and a letter describing their interest in the position. This generally would not apply to me, but for the line in the memo included the opportunity for qualified captains to apply. A voice inside of me says, "The chief is talking about you." Now I start to have one of those internal conversations. I'm thinking, *What! Talking about me? I just underperformed during the major's test, and now I'm just going to hurdle over the battalion chief's position and blast right up to assistant chief!? Yeah, right--that's just ridiculous!* I look at the second page of the memorandum, and it communicates the job description and duties of the assistant chief of administration and support services. As I read over the description that highlights the extensive responsibilities of this assistant chief, that voice speaks up again and says, "This job description is describing you perfectly! You could put your picture on this job description!"

This time I don't argue with the inner voice; I am in full agreement. This describes every skill, proficiency, and expertise that I have gained in my seventeen years of directing three non-profit organizations and two start-up businesses. It's like the chief took my specialties and made them the job requirements. Nonetheless, I'm still not convinced to apply. I print a copy of the memorandum and place it neatly in my take-home bag; I need a few days to think about this. I tell my wife about the memorandum, the job description, and the opportunity. She tries to advise me of how perfect I will be for the position, and how she thinks that I will be a terrific addition to the chief's staff. But I don't believe her. *I think, I can't go by what she says. She's my wife, and she is completely biased in my favor.*

The next duty day, as I sit in the captain's office, I pull the memo out, look at it one last time, and then ball it up and throw it in the trash basket. But, no sooner does it leave my hands than the voice speaks up again. "If you don't at least apply, you will never know what could happened." And that is the truth. Remember:

{LESSON 25} "You beat most of the competition just by showing up!"

Most people are too afraid, too insecure, too filled with doubt and unbelief that they never pursue the possibilities, never go after the opportunities that life presents. I decide to pull the memorandum out of the trash can and go after the possibility sitting in front of me. I update my resume, compose my interest letter and forward both to the chief. After I send the letter in, I don't tell anyone that I am even considering such drastic promotion. Experience has taught me:

{LESSON 28} "Most people won't go after their own opportunities, so they will try and convince you why you shouldn't go after yours."

Plus, I am already struggling with my confidence and faith; I don't need anybody else to share their doubts and negativity. Nearly two weeks pass, and finally I receive a memo from the chief's office announcing the date and time of my interview with the chief. When I read it, my stomach starts to hurt, and I almost changed my mind. I started "sour grapeing" the opportunity, telling myself, "The chief probably already has someone that he's going to promote and that I'm going to be doing all of this studying and preparation for nothing." But I decide that since I had come this far, I might as well see it to the end.

The interview day comes quickly, and I find myself in the waiting area sitting on the bench that is known as the "Hot

Seat." It is where everyone has sat each time they come to headquarters for any interview situation (new hire candidate, promotional, or disciplinary interviews). I have sat in the "Hot Seat" five times in my career, but today the seat seems to have been heated seven times hotter. The chief's secretary informs me that he is ready for me. I had never been to the chief's office before this, and I am impressed by the substantial size and the distinguished décor of the office.

The chief is very cordial and welcoming. "Come on in, Michael, and have a seat." The chief is sitting in a massive executive-style chair that looks big enough to fit four people in it. He is sitting behind an oak wood desk the size of a small dance floor, and he asks me, "Michael, are you a little nervous?"

I respond, "No sir, Chief. I am a whole lot nervous."

The chief laughs and responds, "Well, just relax and let's get started."

He tells me that he has about twenty-five questions, and starts right into asking the first one. He asks me questions concerning leadership style, communication plans, employee discipline, and administration practices. As I am presenting my answers, the chief is busy taking notes of the highlights of my statements, and nodding his head in approval. After about twenty questions, he sits up, leans back in his massive chair, looks into the air and in the middle of the interview says, "Michael Ford."

Then I'm thinking, *The way he just said my name, I think the chief is actually considering me!*

He continues with questions regarding budgeting processes and practices, human resources, grant writing, construction projects, and employment law. As I am presenting these answers, the chief again is busy taking notes of the highlights of my statements, and nodding his head in approval. Again, he sits up, leans back in his massive chair, looks into the air and in the middle of the interview says, "Michael Ford, Michael Ford."

Again, I'm thinking, *The way he just said my name twice, I think the chief is actually considering me!* He asks me about the details of my resume, and about the organizations that I have led, and the teams that I have built. He then asks me how I think that I will manage in the position of assistant chief of administration and support services. I explain my organizational experience of building people and teams and working with diverse entities and agencies. As we close the interview, the chief tells me that he had previously not known much about me, and that he is glad that I have applied. The interview went so well, that I actually think there is a significant chance that I have won the position. I mean, I know that I am still a long shot, because there were ten very strong candidates that interviewed, and most of them are battalion chiefs, but I now feel good about my chances. Nearly three weeks pass without any word on who actually has been chosen. Finally, a new memorandum arrives, announcing that Major Ricky Bobby will be promoted to assistant chief.

Wow. For a moment this news is a punch in my gut; I really started to think that the position might be mine. After the initial disappointment of the news, I experience an overall feeling of satisfaction, knowing that I at least went after a great opportunity. A few weeks later, the chief sends an email to me explaining that he was impressed with my resume and interview, and that he will keep my information on file. I appreciate the note, but I just assume that he sent that note to everyone he interviewed.

A few months go by, I am in-charge of Truck Company 10, and we have just returned to the fire station from grocery shopping, when we notice the chief's vehicle is parked on the station ramp. All of us were wondering why the chief is here at our station. There are twenty-one fire stations in the Louisville Fire Department, and it's a bit unusual for him to just drop by unannounced. So, I look at my three company members and ask, "Okay, which one of you did something so bad that the chief had to personally come and discipline you?"

Everyone laughs and denies any wrongdoing. We park the truck inside the station and all get out and greet the chief. We all stand there laughing and small talking with the chief for nearly twenty minutes. Finally, the chief says, "Well, guys, I have to go, but I need to speak to you, Captain Ford," as he motions for me to follow him into the apparatus bay. As I exit the room to follow the chief, my crew smirks, and gives me the "You've been naughty" look.

The chief walks me to a corner near the bay doors for some privacy and the smile on his face is replaced by a more serious "let's get down to business" look, and he says, "Mike, one of my assistant chiefs just retired unexpectedly. I could open the position and entertain additional interviews, but I was impressed with you when you came up to interview. Now, if you are still interested, I would like to offer the position to you."

Wow! I am completely stunned! I want to have a clever answer and maybe even play it a bit cool, but before I can speak, I need to pick up my eyes, nose, ears, and mouth from off the floor. Finally, I tell the chief that I would be honored to accept the position. I ask him, when would I start? He explains, that he wants me to start on Monday. Wow! Today is Friday, and he wants me to start on Monday! What can happen in a day, a major life's promotion can happen in a day! The chief clarifies a few more details; I shake his hand and thank him for the opportunity, and within a few moments, he leaves. I am so jubilant that I don't know what to do! I rush back toward the captain's office; I have to tell someone the good news, because I am about to burst!

I reach for my cell phone and immediately call my wife. "I have some news! But you need to be sitting down for this one!" She tries to ask me a question, but my tone and excitement are so erratic that she can't tell if something is right or wrong. I interrupt, "You won't believe what just happened! Are you sitting down?!"

She replies, "No, I'm not sitting down because you are making me nervous! What happened?!"

"Okay, okay! Do you remember the position that I interviewed for, a few months ago?"

She says, "Yes, the assistant chief position that you didn't get."

"Yes, that one! Well, today when we got back from the store, we found the chief waiting inside the station! The chief just pulled me to the side and told me that one of the assistant chiefs just retired! He said that he could open the position up for further interviews, but he feels good about selecting someone from the recent interviews. So, guess what! He says he wants me to take the position and he wants me to start on Monday!"

My wife laughs out loud with excitement as she asks, "Wait, are you playing? Are you serious?!"

I tell her that I am not playing and I am not joking; I am very serious. She then expresses how happy she is for me. "I wish I was there to hug you and congratulate you in person. I am really proud of you. The chief picked the right person--you are going to do great."

I thank her, tell her I love her, and end the call. I then call my mom and dad and tell them the sensational news; they both are extremely proud of me. You know, one of my life's most enjoyable pleasures is making my parents proud of me. After these initial calls, I start wondering who else I am supposed to call. The chief never mentioned whether he is going to send out a department-wide memorandum, announcing my new assignment. Well, I think it prudent to at least notify my current supervisor. I call Battalion 4--it is Major Rout. During various parts of my career, he has served as my captain, my union president, and now my battalion chief. When he picks up the phone, I identify myself and tell him that I won't be reporting to my assigned company on Monday.

He asks, "Michael will you be on trade or on a vacation day?"

I reply, "No, sir. I will be detailed to headquarters."

He quickly interrupts with, "Why?"

I explain that I have just been asked by the chief to take the position of assistant chief. Major Rout goes silent for a moment, I think to process the news that I just dropped in his ears. He softly responds, "Well, Michael, I guess that will make you my boss."

Not wanting to show any disrespect to a man that I have a lot of respect for, I respond back with, "Well, I guess, technically."

He then asks, "Well, I hope I have been good to you?"

With a bit of an embarrassing laugh, I respond, "You certainly have, sir."

He graciously congratulates me. I humbly thank him, and we end the call. For the next five years, I serve as assistant chief in one of the department's most successful executive staffs in the history of the department. This staff is able to accomplish goals that made Louisville Fire one of the most well-respected departments in the country. When I think about the success that we have experienced, I often think back to the two days that brought me to this position. First, of course, the day that the chief stopped by my fire station to see me and offered me the assistant chief's position. Second, but most important, the day the position opening memorandum arrived at my desk. That day brought fourth such an important and significant moment, where a personal decision had to be made.

I had to decide whether I was going to apply for the position or allow my fears, insecurities and what other people thought or would say hinder me from accepting the challenge of a new opportunity. I have often thought, "What would have happened if I had given in to my fears and insecurities? The answer, "Nothing!" Nothing would have happened, I would have never known the accomplishments of the past five years. I would have never developed the beautiful workplace relationships, nor reaped the tremendous financial benefits, and the wealth of experience that came with this position.

The truth is, anything can happen in a day, but we have the power to steer the day in our favor by the way we spend and utilize the 24 hours that each day supplies.

{LESSON 29} "Going after a new opportunity, a dream, or a set goal can be intimidating and awfully scary, but the alternative of never experiencing life's possibilities is totally unacceptable."

{LESSON 30} "The truth is, anything can happen in a day, but we have the power to steer the day in our favor with the wisdom and an attitude that is set and determined to succeed and to cherish every 24 hours that each day supplies."

Thank you for taking this journey with me through some of the 24-hour days of my 23-year career in the fire service. I hope you have enjoyed and gleaned knowledge from some of the stories of tragedy, adventure, mishap and triumph that I have shared. Many of my readers are themselves firefighters and emergency services employees and family members. I would love for you to share your stories of service, adventure, comedy, and family with me and the world. Simply go to WWW.MichaelFordJr.com, and add your short story to the link "Additional Stories." Your story will be reviewed and possibly added to the site or it may even be included in my next book.

I look forward to hearing from you.

Please remember to purchase copies of this book as gifts for friends and family. This is a fun book to read for all ages.

Michael Ford Jr.

Bibliography

Aurora Regional Fire Museum . (2009, 9 30). *Firefighting in the Horse-Drawn Era - Getting There (K3 001)*, video. (A. R. Museum, Producer, and Aurora Regional Fire Museum) Retrieved 1 1, 2018, from Youtube: https://youtu.be/n5GWgDOgfYQ

Balch, R. A. (1954). *The Pledge of Allegiance of the United States*. Retrieved January 1, 2018, from Wikipedia: https:/en.m.wikipedia.org/wiki/Pledge_of_Allegiance_(United_States)

Bible . (n.d.). In *James 4:14*. New King James Version.

David. (n.d.). Psalms 30:5. In *Bible*. King James.

Ditko, S. L. (1962, August 1). Spider-Man. *Marvel Comics*. USA: Marvel Comics.

Gene Roddenberry, R. B. (Producer), and Gene Roddenberry, R. B. (Writer). (1987-1994). *Star Trek - Next Generation and Voyager* [Motion Picture]. USA: CBS Television Distribution.

Jeanne Segal, P. L. (2017, October 21). *HELPGUIDE.ORG - Trusted guide to mental and emotional health.* Retrieved January 5, 2018, from HELPGUIDE.ORG: https://www.helpguide.org/articles/mental-health/laughter-is-the-best-medicine.htm

LeRoy, M. (Producer), Baum, L. F. (Writer), and Fleming, V. (Director). (8/25/1939). *The Wizard of Oz* [Motion Picture]. United States: Loew's Inc.

Longaberger, H. (2012, January 1). *Famous Horses in History.* Retrieved January 5, 2018, from Equitrekking. com: http://www.equitrekking.com/articles/entry/famous_horses_in_history_-_the_fire_horse/

Matthew Vaughn, D. R. (Producer), Vaughn, J. G. (Writer), and Vaughn, M. (Director). (2014). *Kingsman - Secret Service* [Motion Picture]. USA and United Kingdom: 20th Century Fox.

Matthew, S. (n.d.). St. Matthew. In S. Matthew, *Bible.*

Paramedic, M. M. (n.d.). *Dalmatian Dog* . Retrieved January 5, 2018, from Dalmatian dog From Wikipedia, the free encyclopedia (Redirected from Dalmatian (dog): http://www.publicsafety.net/dalmatian.htm

Paul. (n.d.). Ephesians 4:26 NIV. In Paul, *Bible.*

Sally C. Curtin, M. M. (2016, April 1). *NCHS Data Brief No. 241 April 2016 Centers for Disease Control and Prevention's (CDC) National Center for Health Statistics 1999–2014 multiple cause-of-death mortality files* . Retrieved November 1, 2017, from www.cdc.gov: https://www.cdc.gov/nchs/products/databriefs/db241.htm

Weintraub, J. (Producer), Kamen, R. M. (Writer), and
    Avildsen, J. G. (Director). (1984). *The Karate Kid*
    [Motion Picture]. USA: Columbia Pictures.

CPSIA information can be obtained
at www.ICGtesting.com
Printed in the USA
BVHW03s1838231018
531018BV00001B/34/P